Best of Our Memoirs

Contributing Writers

Lita Askanas

Dorothy Atkins

Mabel Brix

Grace Bush

Loraine Campbell

Chuck Chaffin

Diana Chan

Debby Freeman

Joan Gomersall

Luanna Leisure

Carol McFarlin

Jim Oggerino

Norma Slavit

Dee Steward

Jing-Shio Su

Dick Walthart

Louise Webb

Compiled by
Luanna K. Lynch Leisure

Best of Our Memoirs

This special dedication honors our memoirs leader, Louise Webb, who is our inspiration! Thank you for your enthusiasm, dedication and continued support, and thank you for teaching us to, "Always add a quote to every memoir you write." We are all better by being a part of your class.

Cover photo by Luanna K. Lynch Leisure
Taken in San Jose, California

Best of Our Memoirs

Louise Webb's Memoirs Class
February 27, 2008
Photo taken after a presentation at the
Saratoga Senior Center

Front row: Lita Askanas, Louise Webb, Jeanne Roths,
Cecilia Frizell, Charlotte Vukelick, Joan Gomersall, Jane Stewart,
Mabel Brix, Loraine Campbell, Ginny Johnson.
Back row: Dee Steward, Jim Oggerino, Jo Mary Keith,
Max Van Rhee.

Contents

Contents

Contents

Contents

Acknowledgements

Sincerest gratitude goes to all of those who have participated in creating, *Best of Our Memoirs.*

Debby Freeman: For making calls, interviewing and collecting memoirs.

Grace Bush: For interviewing and collecting memoirs.

Jing-Shio Su: For interviewing and collecting memoirs.

Joan Gomersall: For collecting memoirs.

Norma Slavit: For her hours of proofreading.

Herb Leisure: For his proofreading and kind encouragement.

To all of our class, THANK YOU for sharing
your memoirs. Without you, this book
would not be possible.

What is Your Memoir?

When I first started attending Louise Webb's memoirs class, and I listened to what the members read about themselves, I realized I did not have to start writing from the day I was born and then proceed writing my life in chronological order.

Each person read about their life, but their stories were never boring, but rather, interesting, intriguing, sad, triumphant, funny sometimes shocking and personal. I could relate to so many of them, and because of their kindness and acceptance, it was easy for me to share my life.

Many times, while writing about a specific event in my life, I would call my sister, Sharyl, and ask her if she remembered it in the same way. Many times she would agree, but just as many times she had a different view. This is okay. My sister is four years older and her perception and experiences are not and cannot be the same as mine. From her point of view she may have understood the event in a different way. There are so many variables that can cause different people to be at the same place at the same time and have conflicting opinions on what happened.

What each person has to do is honestly relate, in their own personal memoir, their own experience and perception. Sometimes my sister and I have different opinions but we can also be positive that each of us is correct in our own personal observation.

So, what is your memoir? Don't be afraid to start writing for fear of getting the facts wrong. Write as honestly as you possibly can and do your research. What I discovered to be most exciting as I wrote, was the clarity that began to appear in my mind. Events would fall into place. My memory would be sparked by a trigger of remembrance.

I discovered that not only do you begin to understand yourself better but more ideas and situations come to the surface. It can be extremely healing and exciting.

Memoirs can also be written in poetry. If a poem comes to mind about an event, and that is the style you desire to use, then it is completely acceptable. It is still your memoir.

Memoirs are non-fiction. Does that mean one cannot take some fact from life, draw upon that fact and turn it into a fictional story? Of course we can.

I have written three children's books and in all three I have taken excerpts from my life, exaggerated, embellished and turned these events upside down and created fiction. What's fun is no one knows what is fact or fiction. I wouldn't doubt it if most fiction writers glean part of their material from real-life experiences.

But, most importantly, our memoirs are non-fiction.

If you are reading this book, you may be interested in writing your own memoirs. I encourage you to do so. Read what our class has written. Most of us are not professional writers, but we do appreciate and enjoy reading our stories and listening to each other, as well as give each other helpful suggestions.

Check your local community center or senior center for a memoirs class. Our class meets at the Saratoga Senior Center in Saratoga, California. You may enjoy attending.

If you are staring at a blank computer screen and don't know how to get started writing, just read the memoirs in this book. Also, in the back is a listing of topics that may help trigger some ideas.

What is *your* memoir?

Luanna K. Lynch Leisure

Jayne Meadows

Bob Mackie

PRESS

Red Skelton

Jim Cameron

Oprah Winfrey

Ann Jillian

Jimmy Durante

Richard Simmons

Peggy Fleming

Olivia de Havilland

Elizabeth Gilbert

Willie Nelson

Vanna White

Wally Amos

Louise King Webb

I have been writing my memoirs and leading a memoirs class for over 16 years. The students are ambitious and make me proud.

My college education includes Indiana University and National College of Education in Evanston. After teaching for a few years, I returned and earned my Master's Degree in Education at National College of Education. It was during this time when I met my husband, Ian, who was attending Northwestern University. I began my career as a fourth grade teacher in Riverside, California, subsequently teaching in Hawaii, Santa Barbara, France and Saratoga.

After rearing our daughter, I started a new career as a freelance writer and columnist for the Saratoga News. During my twenty year career as a Celebrity Journalist, I had the privilege of interviewing many well-known and prestigious individuals including Elizabeth Taylor, Willie Nelson, Oprah Winfrey, Olivia de Havilland, Truman Capote, Richard Simmons, Bruce (Caitlin) Jenner, Clint Eastwood, Vanna White, Lena Horne, Jimmy Carter and Gerald Ford. Erma Bombeck once saw some of my writings and wrote, "She has charisma." For many years I attended the Oscars to interview the stars.

Running in marathons used to be one of my hobbies. I ran in Hawaii and in Russia. These accomplishments changed me. Other hobbies include photography, world travel, collecting and wearing pretty hats.

Achievements include a special award given twice by the Saratoga City Council for leading Random Acts of Kindness week. In 2016 two of my memoirs were featured in a book called, *My Life, My Story My Legacy.*

I am a member of the National League of American Pen Women, Santa Clara Branch, California Writer's Club, the Foothill Club, Saratoga Sister City, Friends of the Library, Valley Women's League, Hakone, Saratoga Assistant League and the AAUW.

My volunteer work includes the Saratoga Book-Go-Round, and Adult Care through the Los Gatos and Saratoga Assistance League.

I also have an identical twin sister, Susan Gaede, of Southern California, who, just like me, taught fourth grade and wrote as a columnist.

Jimmy the Bus Driver

by Louise Webb

Middle-age Jimmy was our bus driver in Evanston, Illinois. I always looked forward to seeing him. He loved kids but didn't have any of his own. "You are my children," he said to us. My treasured friend put our photos up and we felt important.

Adults also rode the bus. The driver trusted the adults and they would get on either from the front or back and would pay their fares as they left the bus.

Jimmy would even make the bus dance by turning the wheels from side to side, and he would hold up an umbrella as if the bus was dancing with the umbrella. He only did this once in a while when we were in a safe place. We thought it was magical.

Another time the bus stopped at the train tracks and a man in a car next to us tried to beat the train. We saw the man's head fly off. Jimmy tried to calm us. I still remember the scene vividly.

The bus driver used to sing to me, "Every little breeze whispers Louise." I liked the words and the attention until I was older. It then became an embarrassment. I didn't tell Jimmy how I felt because it would have hurt his feelings.

He got sick and a substitute driver took his place. The new driver was shocked that people were getting on the front and back door and paying later. He reported it to the bus company and Jimmy was fired. Things were never the same. We all missed our Jimmy.

The Weirdest Thing I Ever Saw

by Louise Webb

When asked about what was the weirdest thing I ever saw, I thought of the man's head flying off in the convertible next to our bus. I was five years old and the horrible scene still sticks in my mind like it just happened.

Another incident that stands out as unusual is seeing Siamese twins in person. I had experienced glimpses of life as a Siamese twin when my identical twin sister, Sue, and I portrayed Siamese twins in a college circus musical.

We called several clothing stores to see if any of them had a size 52 dress. I don't know how we came up with that number, but we felt two of us could get in that size dress. Sale clerks giggled when we asked for that size dress and then they tried to stifle their giggles and be polite. Finally, we found a few stores that carried a size 52. A long dress was needed to cover our legs. We each stuck one of our arms out and sang a lyric asking the audience for advice. "What would you do if one liked to stay home and the other one liked to roam?"

We had hats hidden on our backs and brought them out in the end deciding two hats were better than one because with two hats we didn't have to choose which one we liked best.

Dress rehearsals were not fun. We couldn't sit in the auditorium chairs. I remember wanting a drink and realized I needed Sue's cooperation. She wanted to finish her homework and didn't want to get a drink with me. I had to plead.

Jokingly we tried to enroll in our next semester classes as one person. The registrar didn't think it was funny. Our friends thought it was hilarious.

Years later a set of real 18 year old Siamese twins were at a San Francisco television station and Sue and I were attending the broadcast. The interviewer, Steve, came out beforehand and chatted. It was apparent how much he adored the Siamese twins. "I took them dancing until the wee hours of the night last night," he informed us and he had tears in his eyes.

"They are from a poor, large family, and I went out and bought the girls a wardrobe of clothes," Steve added. "The family wants to protect them from being called freaks and keep people from staring."

The twins are home-schooled. (I could identify with people staring at twins but we just got used to it.) I am sure in their case there would be more gawking. The emcee said they were used to their church family and did go to church where they sang many duets. He pointed out this was their first outing besides church and even though they lived near Disneyland they had never been.

He then brought the girls out. They were clutching dolls. The audience gasped but the Siamese twins immediately put us all at ease with their winning smiles and outgoing personalities. They were obviously very comfortable in their own skins and answered all our curious questions such as; "If doctors could separate the two of you would you like it?" The answer in unison was a definite "no." "Would they like to be married some day?" "No," again, they said and added, "We have each other."

Steve told them he was going to take them to Disneyland. They were extremely excited and I think after this first exposure in San Francisco they were ready for stares and perhaps some name calling.

I thought about them often and a few years later I came across their obituary in the newspaper. They lived several more years and after their first steps with Steve and Disneyland I hope they had many more chances to broaden their lives.

Ann Sheridan

by Louise Webb

Recently I spotted an old photo of Ann Sheridan. A Hollywood studio once named her the "Oomph Girl." Her picture was posted in the hallway of an old Berkeley City Club building and the snapshot brought back memories.

Teresa Young, a classmate of mine l I knew back in grade school, happened to write the millionth fan letter to Miss Sheridan. As a result, the youngster was chosen to go to Hollywood to meet Ann. Teresa became a local celebrity in my hometown of Evanston, Illinois, where we both lived.

She was a shy little girl and was overwhelmed with the sudden media blast, but also was enjoying her new found fame. Teresa was asked to be a model and her picture continuingly appeared in our local newspapers. She seemed to blossom overnight with all the attention.

The local media kept us up to date on Teresa's adventures, even letting the town know that Ann found Teresa adorable. Teresa would be staying in Hollywood longer because Ann was going to put her in some scenes in her upcoming film. My friends and I were happy for her and also jealous.

I had written long fan letters to Rita Hayworth, Margaret O'Brien, June Allyson and others before Teresa wrote to Ann Sheridan. Each letter was different and I put a lot of effort into them. After searching the mail box daily for several weeks I finally got photos back of all three stars.

"Look, Sue," I showed my twin proudly. "I got autograph photos of every movie star I wrote." When I smeared the signatures and the ink didn't smudge, I realized the signatures were stamped. That was the last time I wrote a fan letter to a celebrity. Why couldn't I have had Teresa's luck?

Serita Krop

by Louise Webb

She was a high school model and walked like one. Serita Krop had all kinds of titles, some big and a few I didn't understand like, "Miss Sidewalk."

I was pleased I was going to be seen with "Miss Sidewalk." We were going to a Friday night basketball game together to watch her boyfriend, Mike, play. The young athlete had flaming red hair with freckles to match. Serita and Mike were in love and going steady.

When we left our house to go to the basketball tournament, Serita had on a new, beautiful blue, angora sweater. A string of shiny pearls were nestled around her neck. Her saddle shoes looked like they had just been polished. She had soft, dark curls and long dark eyelashes. I got a whiff her fragrant perfume.

We got to the gym early so Serita could have a good seat and yell encouraging words to Mike. This was an important game because the team had made the finals.

Her boyfriend was playing well in the first few quarters. Serita was thrilled. The scores were close. Mike threw the ball breaking a tie. Serita stood up yelling cheering words as loud as she could but something was wrong. People were giggling. The impossible had happened. He had thrown the ball in the wrong basket. Making matters worse, the coach immediately took Mike out of the game. The crowd applauded him for his efforts. He turned red matching his hair.

Serita was furious. "How could you be so stupid and embarrass me?" She yelled.

It wasn't any fun being with Serita for the rest of the game. I looked at Serita in a different way after seeing her behave so badly. I thought to myself, "Maybe it is the inner beauty that really counts."

Broken Prom Date

by Louise Webb

I took a speech class with Miss Anderson in my senior year at high school. Louie Polydoris sat across the aisle from me. I had seen Louie before but had never met him. He had a reputation of being well-liked. Louie reminded me of a cocker spaniel with his curly dark hair and big brown eyes. He looked like he wanted to be cuddled.

The second time the class met he suggested at the end of it, "Let's make it a Lou Lou and go out, okay?" (People called me Lou rather than Louise in high school because my twin's name was Sue and we had rhyming names Sue and Lou).

The teacher overheard Louie ask me out and she apparently thought we were a cute couple because she encouraged the romance by always handing back my papers to Lou to give to me and vice versa.

Louie and I dated several times. I could tell he thought he was in love with me because he had that puppy love look about him when he was courting me. I wasn't as smitten, but I thought he was fun. My friends liked him and my "Y" Club chose him as our mascot.

One date night stood out with Louie. We went on a high school hay ride with several friends. It was a beautiful November evening but chilly. Louie and I snuggled and he kept me warm. Both of us enjoyed the starry out door airy night. The group sang songs while the horses paraded and pulled the cart. Louie commented, "This has been the best night of my life!"

The prom was far off but I thought this might be the time to hint, "I wonder if the prom could be this wonderful?" Louie got the message and popped the question.

"Will you go with me to the prom?" He asked in an excited tone. "Of course," I said. It was a done deal.

We continued dating and it was obvious he was in love. I was not and took Louie somewhat for granted. Then suddenly we weren't dating. I heard he was seeing Beverly Vaughn, an attractive teenager. I wasn't too concerned because he told one of my friends he was still taking me to the prom. A few months later, Louie told someone that Beverly dangled her feet out the window. Lou would never do that. He was right I wouldn't think of rolling down the window and dangling my feet out the window.

I bought a prom dress with a silk top and netted skirt. A few days later a friend had a difficult time telling me that Louie had told her he was going to break the prom date with me but asked her if she would please tell me first. Hearing the news I felt like I had been kicked in the stomach. The days rolled by and we still sat next to each other in class and Miss Anderson continued to give Louie my papers to give me and vice versa.

One day I saw Louie in the hallway. "Would you still like to go with me to the prom? I mean . . ." He stammered and I knew what he really meant. He no longer wanted to go to the prom with me and was self-conscious trying to break the date when the two of us were alone. I let him have it.

"My sister is going to the prom. I have my dress and now I am not going. But what is even worse is how you turned out to be." I blurted out, and as I walked away I saw guilt written all over his face.

My "Y" Club was angry with Louie when they heard what he did they gave him the cold shoulder and Louie was no longer our mascot. I appreciated my friend's support.

People were excited that the prom was coming soon. Someone said Ted Wandberg was going to take a senior because he thought it was only right. I said, "What a lucky girl who gets to go with Ted." He was a handsome guy and special. In the fourth grade I had a movie date with Ted and paid my own way on the bus, three cents each way.

One day Ted stopped me in the hall and asked me to the prom. I was in total shock and screamed, "Yes," so loudly that I think the school walls vibrated and almost scared the poor boy.

Prom night was a memorable night for me after all. Ted evidently didn't know anything about what Louie had put me through because he stopped and chatted with Louie and Beverly much to the embarrassment of the three of us. (I gloated inside).

Years later I attended our high school class reunion. Louie came over to meet my knight in shining armor, Ian. He told us he had since had two divorces, was still a louse, and I was much better off with Ian than himself. Miss Anderson probably thought for years that Louie and I were a married couple who had met in her classroom.

Shirley Temple

by Louise Webb

She was the little girl with dimples and curly hair who captured the hearts of the nation. Numerous Mothers tried to make their daughters look like her, act like her, and dance like her but there was only one Shirley Temple.

Shirley Temple

The first time I saw Shirley I literally bumped into her in Santa Barbara at the Biltmore Hotel where she was the guest speaker. I asked the star if I could take her picture. She graciously said, "Yes." Several times I tried but the flash wouldn't go off. Finally I had to give up. When she was introduced at the podium I was amazed and impressed at her long list of accomplishments that had nothing to do with Hollywood. The starlet was a huge volunteer.

After the program, I followed the photographers who were taking pictures of her and luck was with me, the flash finally went off. "Shirley, it worked," I called out, and she showed those famous Shirley dimples in response. The shot turned out great and years later I sent her two copies one for her to sign and one for her to keep. The photos were not returned.

I never dreamed then that I would be interviewing Shirley in the future. Many years later, after I had moved to Northern California, I read in the paper she was to be the guest on the TV show, *People*

Are Talking in San Francisco. I called the station for a ticket and I was informed there were 100 people already on the waiting list but I decided to take the risk and go anyway.

"Does anyone have an extra ticket?" I asked the people who were lined up with tickets in hand. A man towards the front did and I stood with him. It was announced that the first 6 people would sit in the front row. My number was a 9 but I realized if I turned it around the number magically turned into a 6.

I overheard the producers discussing that Shirley was signing books at a San Francisco Book Store after the show. I decided to go and when I was there I asked her press agent if I could have an interview with the famous icon.

"I will have Shirley call you," she answered. "Wow," I thought to myself, "Shirley Temple is going to call me, but what if I'm not home?"

"How about if I interview her after the book signing?" I asked quickly. The press agent said she would try to arrange it and she did.

It was turning into my lucky day. I stood with Shirley's husband, Charles Black, while she signed books. Many of her admirers brought her presents and the press agent brought the gifts over to Charles. He held an arm full of dolls, flowers, etc. Mr. Black and I waited patiently in the corner while Shirley signed the books and talked to her fans. Charles appeared to be shy and I resisted taking his picture holding all the gifts. I had some principles.

After the signing Shirley told me as a youngster she wasn't aware of her popularity. She said a lot of young people still think of her as a little girl and are disappointed to see her all grown up. Shirley said she preferred to be called Mrs. Black instead of Shirley Temple. Mrs. Black talked about her husband in glowing terms. She was shorter in height than I expected.

I talked to her at another book signing in Campbell, California and had a copy of the picture I had mailed to her. This was 30 years later. "Tell me that picture was taken recently. Right?" she kidded as she sipped a nutritious drink during the signing.

The fourth time I saw Shirley was when someone invited me to a Republican Garden Party event in Palo Alto where she was again a guest speaker. People thought Shirley would be roaming around the garden and they could speak to her freely, but that wasn't the case. She spoke and then went into the guest house on the grounds. Fortunately for me, a gal in charge of the event recognized me in the audience earlier and came out and said they needed a photographer. "Would you please come in and take pictures?" she asked. I said, "I would!"

When I went in the house Shirley was standing with an armful of beautiful flowers she had received earlier from the chairman of the event. "I'm allergic to roses," she commented and proceeded to dump them in a nearby waste basket. I saw a peek of the human side of Shirley Temple that day.

Twins and Their Dates

by Louise Webb

I just finished reading a book titled, *The Lives of Twins* by Rosamond Smith. It turned out that the author's real name was Joyce Carol Oates. Her book was fiction about a set of twin men who dated the same woman. The twin that the woman had moved in with didn't know she had started seeing his twin brother. She had arranged to meet his brother out of curiosity and ended up falling in love with both twins.

Louise and Susan
(Lou and Sue)

There was a period of time when I had my identical twin on a pedestal. The man I was dating at the time had never met Sue, my twin. My male friend told me after meeting her that he was scared he would fall in love. He said he was in love with me and I described her in such glowing terms he thought she must be even better than I was. After meeting her he was thankful he liked me the best.

I soon realized being a twin can create problems which could affect others. Years later, while living in Hawaii, I ran into Dick, a man I had previously dated. He told me when my twin was at the same party and I would go in the other room he felt inadequate. "Which one was his date?" he wondered. Dick had to ask other people to find out which twin I was so he would make sure and take home the right girl.

Sometimes we took advantage of the situation. If we were going on double blind dates one was usually better than the other and we had an agreement to switch dates half way through the evening. The only problem was we didn't know what the other had asked his date and we found ourselves asking the new date the same questions the other twin had already asked.

One day Sue called me and said she had a date Thursday night with John Black. I said, "I have a date with John Black Thursday night." I thought he was a little bold because he just told me the day and time he was picking me up without asking if I was available. We decided to call John and find out who had the date. John was embarrassed and said he would go with Sue and get me a date with his friend Kaye and we would double date.

"We better wear our Sue and Lou name sweaters," I said to Sue. We went to the Commons, a local Indiana University hangout. By coincidence there were only men there that evening. Sue and I happen to pick up our utensils in unison constantly while we were eating. Everyone in the place watched. The four of us felt self-conscious because we were aware everyone was staring.

John and Kaye left us to get more cokes at the bar. Two new boys entered the Commons and came over to Sue and me asking if they could join us. Others in the Commons knew we already had been taken that evening and watched the scenario with amusement. It was like a floor show going on. Sue once dated someone much later who had been there that night and said he would never forget it. Yes, being twins does call attention!

One evening I made two dates in one night but spaced them out. I thought I could get away with it. It turned out they weren't spaced far enough. My date had told me he had to get in by a certain time or he would get fraternity demerits. It was getting very late, and I was getting nervous. I reminded him about the demerits. "You're worth it," he told me. Just as I was kissing him goodnight my date walked in and I said, "I will tell my twin you're here." I quickly changed clothes and came out again. It worked!

When Ian, my husband, and I were going together and my twin came two days early for a visit, I sent her down stairs and had her pretend she was me. She fooled him for awhile until she began talking with a Southern accent. Sue had been stationed with her husband in the South and had picked up a Southern accent. He was sorry to this day he didn't take her off to the movies and leave me behind!

Ending My Writing Career as a Reporter After an Interview with Debbie Reynolds

by Louise Webb

I read in the paper that Debbie Reynolds was speaking at the San Jose Fairmount for a benefit. Hurriedly, I got in my car and drove to the Fairmount well before the event started. "I am from the Saratoga News. Is it possible to get an interview with Miss Reynolds?" I asked one of the sponsors. She was delighted and told me I was the only reporter and wanted me to ask Debbie lots of questions.

Debbie Reynolds

I was escorted by the sponsor in a private elevator that I didn't know existed. It wasn't long before I was face to face with the star, her entourage, and a spattering of people associated with the event.

The talented celebrity looked perky, young for her age, and very stylish in her silk, V-necked dress. After I was introduced to her the first thing she did was jump on a table and cross her legs in a sexy pose while I snapped pictures. I kept firing questions. Debbie was proud that her daughter, Carrie, had become well known as Princess Leia in the movie, Star Wars Trilogy. Debbie loved it when fans asked her, "Are you Princess Leia's Mother?"

As I was interviewing Debbie about her varied career I couldn't help flashing back on a memory of another time when I saw her in person. It was when our family was living in Santa Barbara. My daughter, Patty, now 50 years old, was then only five. Debbie was signing shoes in a shoe store that her then husband, Harry Karl, owned. I bought Patty a white pair of tennis shoes and Debbie leaned down to sign the new shoes on my daughter's feet. "Look, Mommy, she has a wiglet on just like yours," my daughter shouted out. Wiglet hair pieces were very popular back then. I was embarrassed!!

If a little birdie had whispered in my ear in that Santa Barbara shoe store, 30 years later, that I would be interviewing Debbie I would never have believed it. I retired as a reporter from the newspaper after her interview. It seems appropriate that Debbie was my last interview.

Age Is Just a Number

by Louise Webb
1994

I am going to be 60 years old this month. My identical twin, Susan, will be 54. Figure that one out. She came from Southern California to celebrate our 50th, since her friends didn't know it was the big 50, I tricked her by putting 100 candles on the cake! Our birthday is June 14 – flag day. When we were younger and saw all the flags up, we thought everyone was celebrating our birthday.

Friends tell me I look like 50. Perhaps our society needs to change their attitude on aging. I have accepted becoming 60 and like to think in terms of what I read in a book once: "Old age is 10 years older than you are."

I feel young in spirit and happy to have the years of experience behind me. Sometimes there are hints that I am growing older. On Monday mornings it takes all six of my walking friends to remember what the three stories were on *60 Minutes* the night before!

Some people have trouble turning 40. When I was 39 I couldn't wait to be 40 after reading a book titled, *Life Begins at 40*. The jogging craze became popular when I was in my 40s, and I started running marathons including ones in Hawaii and Russia, and ran throughout New Zealand. My husband and daughter thought I was crazy but were supportive.

Towards the end of my 40s and 50s, journalism became important. My first Saratoga News article was about a Caribbean exercise cruise with Richard Simmons. Richard and I helped turn around the thinking of my suicidal roommate.

On the way to Machu Picchu in South America last summer, I was taking pictures of boulders that railroad strikers had placed in front of our train. Men removed the boulders more quickly than I expected, and the train started going. I jumped on the train in motion but I slipped underneath. Fortunately, I was able to spring from underneath back onto the door of the train!

After that experience, I realized more than ever life is a precious gift. I plan to select my choices wisely, have fun, risk and keep changing. At 59, I started wearing bows and hats.

Move over, Shirley MacLaine, Shirley Temple and Liz Taylor; I am in good company and ready to join you.

My Hobbies

by Louise Webb

My overseas travels began when I was twenty- three years old. This is when I started collecting foreign spoons and dolls. Presently I have over 50 spoons from various countries and two-hundred fifty dolls.

I went to Africa and glass, brass, and wooden elephants became my next obsession. Then it was painted eggs. The Russian Church down the street has an annual bazaar and every year I buy a decorated egg.

Joining the Red Hat Society started my hat interest. I have a room full of beautiful hats.

My most unique hobby is collecting Victorian houses. It began one day when I was in San Francisco with my husband and I spotted a blue Victorian house. The house stood out among the others because there was a note on the door and in the mail box was a bouquet of flowers. "What did the note say?" I wondered aloud.

Why the flower bouquet? Had there been a fight between two people? Maybe there was a birthday or an anniversary celebration? If I hadn't been with my hubby, the reporter in me probably would have gotten the best of me and out of curiosity I would have read the note.

When we arrived home I was still curious. "What did the scribbling note mean?" I thought to myself. That evening as I lay in bed I had trouble sleeping thinking again and visualizing the blue Victorian house scene. Was there a secret admirer involved?

The following day I got a canvas and made a Victorian house painting. There was a scribbled note out front and a miniature bouquet. People would have to use their imagination viewing my art work.

The drawing looked lonely by itself. Next, I made a Victorian collage using a San Francisco newspaper. The background was the newspaper and the foreground was a cut out Victorian house. I used hooks and eyes for windows. The door had gold paper.

"Why stop?" I thought. A few days later I baked a cookie in the shape of a Victorian house, painted it and added glaze. A friend got in the act and created a 3 D Victorian house. Others started buying me Victorian house birthday and Christmas gifts.

Where there is a will there is a way. I spotted a Victorian house blender cover in a San Francisco window and managed buying it quickly and caught up with my friends in the next block.

It was in Colorado I saw a large pottery Victorian. The saleslady wouldn't allow me to use my out of state credit card. I skipped lunch and used cash.

My favorite Victorian is a music box that plays 'I left My Heart in San Francisco.' There is a cable car in front and if the string is pulled the cable car will move down the hill.

Every time I am in San Francisco and see Victorians, and even though it was over 45 years ago, I think about the special blue Victorian house and still wonder what the real story was.

Etta Palmer Has Died

by Louise Webb

I have written much about my friend Etta. We were best friends for over 47 years.

It seems strange writing about her in past tense. She died a day after Christmas. It gave me comfort to stroke her hair on Christmas Day and plant a kiss on her forehead. I knew it would be the last time; and I left with a heavy heart saying goodbye to my Etta.

She really wasn't my Etta. There were countless people she inspired such as; Sherpas runners, relatives, friends and strangers. Often I heard her calling out to people during running races that were ready to give up. "You can do it," she would yell in that Southern accent encouraging them. I was one of those people she helped.

The chiropractor told me I couldn't do my first Hawaii marathon due to injuries. Etta took my x-rays to two doctors at Kaiser Hospital, who she worked for, and convinced them to help me get better for the race. They did and I ran the marathon.

I agree with her daughter Maura, who said, "Can't was not in Etta's vocabulary." How many people in this world have started running at 50 years of age and completed 125 26.3 marathons, ran around Lake Tahoe, completed the double dip sea, and numerous other feats. It is not surprising she was chosen Santa Clara Woman of the Year as well as acquiring other awards. Her journey was not an easy one and there were numerous injuries along the way, but like the energizer bunny, she kept going.

Etta was full of serendipities. Some hot days she dropped by bringing me a chocolate yogurt drink. I was a newspaper columnist at the time, and one day I was surprised to read a letter to the editor she had written. It said, "Louise's article she wrote last week should have been on the front page."

I thank you Etta for making me a better person by having known you, and I thank you for going the extra mile in everything you did. It was an honor to be your friend and I will never forget you.

Evanston High School

by Louise Webb

My close friends from Evanston High School in Illinois have met yearly for the last 22 years. This September there were only six of us, and I liked the intimacy of the small group. This was the fourth time we met in Park City, Utah. Bev, a group member, had graciously invited us to stay in her chalet. It sleeps 18 people and we each chose our own room with a shower. The home's interior consisted of unusual woods used for staircase, tables, bed posts, etc. Photographs taken by family members and their own artwork helped create a homey atmosphere.

It doesn't matter which window one looks out. You can see out any window and view the magnificent autumn colors splashed over the mountains. Sometimes there may be a moose or two grazing on the property, deer prancing across the driveway, rabbits running amok or pretty birds flying.

Sue, one of the ladies in our group, gave us a scare this year. She arrived breathless at 6:00 p.m. on the first evening. A few moments later there was a call from her son saying the doctor had phoned. He said Sue's morning tests results showed she should go to the hospital immediately. It was life-threatening. Bev didn't know where the hospital was located since she only uses the chalet part-time but managed to get Sue there in record time. We worried the rest of the evening and following days. It affected our schedule but Sue was our first concern. We were thrilled when she was released two and a half days later and was looking much better.

Bev always manages to find new activities we haven't done. A new experience was a four hour pontoon ride in a State Park reservoir. It was a beautiful day and we brought picnic lunches. Family friends of Bev joined us. The five year old boy tried stuffing the home-made fudge in his mouth and pockets.

The chocolate factory was interesting. We saw how an expensive brand by the name of, Ritual Chocolate, was processed and had eight various samples. I was surprised how many steps were taken involving one bar. We were told by the chocolate connoisseur that chocolate was good for you.

On another day we took a long drive passed Bald Mountain to Lake Miro. Bev and I walked around the lake and had a nice one to one conversation.

A highlight was watching Bev's Granddaughter, Avery, and her boyfriend, Mark practice turns and jumps from a high platform and then land in the water below. They were wearing ski clothes and were on skis. Both are on the Park City Y.S. Olympic team. The couple came to dinner that evening and we plagued them with questions about their sport. Harrietsy, one of our friends in the group, who we refer to as "our indoor chef," helped cook a fancy meal. We went all out with flowers decorating the dining room table.

One lunch we ate outdoors at Leif Erickson's restaurant, named after a famous skier. I had just read in a book by Dr. Ruth that she was a skier but afraid to go down a hill with the champion so he picked her up and carried her on his back going down the hill. She loved it. At a nearby table, Holly met some younger people celebrating a reunion and she encouraged them to keep meeting. Their group enjoyed hearing and seeing how much fun we were having.

The last night we celebrated and had dinner at the well-known Park City's Hotel St. Regis and road the funicular. I don't usually drink but I like ginger and there was a drink called Ginger Mimosa I believe. It turned out not to be a good idea but it did taste good.

Bev has invited us to come back next year. At least one member didn't come this year because she couldn't handle the altitude. We may go to New Orleans and back to Park City the following year.

I had brought books to read but got little reading done. We were busy and having too much fun. Before leaving I saw a quote on a bulletin board in one of the rooms that read, "Friends are like stars. You don't always see them but you know they're always there." I did sit with my close friends in Park City star-gazing at night but now that we have left each other, like the poem says, I still feel their love surrounding me.

Lita Askanas

I first met Louise at the Saratoga High School track. We were both a part of the same walking group and she invited me to attend her memoirs class.

It is difficult to pinpoint which memoir from our group stands out more than the others. Each one meant so much to me. There were so many stories through the years that led me to tears and also joy. There have been so many extraordinary stories. I can't think of just one that had a special meaning for me. The stories have had significant impact on my life.

Judy Oppenheimer's visit to our class was very special. She is now my neighbor. Her life was somewhat traumatic; however, she has risen above all the obstacles in her life.

I feel grateful that I found some talent in being able to express myself.

My Very First Best Friend

by Lita Askansas

I met my future best friend on a Friday afternoon. The sun was shining on a bright October Fall day, the day Rita moved to the same apartment house that I lived in. I saw her standing in front of the lobby. I was curious as to whom this person was who was dressed appropriately in a beige woolen coat with, of all things, a hat to match.

Rita's parents were busy unpacking their things in their new apartment, while, Rita and her sister, Carol waited outside. I was so excited to see someone my age moving in. We became good friends. I always thought that she was much more intelligent than I was, but it didn't bother me. I wasn't the least bit jealous.

Sometimes, on Sunday mornings I had Sunday breakfast with Rita and her family. I would go down to her small apartment and join her family for a delicious breakfast. My family did not allow us to eat bacon and the aroma of bacon in her house made my mouth water.

Rita always looked quite perfect, with every piece of clothing matching—either the correct color coat with the perfect blouse in a similar color and of course, a skirt that went with everything she wore. She always looked so clean. She had pale skin with freckles and her hands were snow white. I even remember feeling that my hands never looked as clean as hers. I think this made her appear superior in my eyes; however, as I said previously, I didn't feel jealous, but I always wondered what she did to make her skin look so clean.

Rita's sister, Carol, was two years younger than we were. She often joined us to play some wonderful games, and we shared extraordinary experiences. These activities always took place in their small apartment. I wonder now why those play times were always in their apartment. We never played in my apartment. As I begin to realize so many things from childhood, I understand that it must have been because I had two brothers, and they wouldn't have understood the importance of our serious female activities.

When we were about six years old, we played house with an elaborate set that consisted of a toy kitchen, a stove, a sink and little chairs around a very small table. An important aspect of our playing house was serving tea to each other. We used miniature cups and saucers, plastic spoons and small plates for cookies. Of course, we served each other empty cups. This was so much fun and, we always dressed up on these occasions.

As we got a little older, around ten years old, we played school. Once again we played in Rita's apartment. We had a large blackboard, chalk, erasers, lined paper and pencils and pens. Each of us took turns being the teacher. Possibly, that is what led us to become teachers. When we played school, I developed a sense of confidence. Being in charge was something unusual for me and I loved giving orders on what they should write and what lessons they were instructed to study. They (Rita and Carol) actually listened to me. Someone listening to my instruction was a first for me.

Rita and I went to the same elementary school, junior high and high school together. Our friendship shifted when we attended different colleges, and we grew somewhat apart. I always felt lucky to have had such an enduring relationship with someone and, that we were able to share our growing up experiences through the years.

Rita's mother and father were quite different than mine. Both of her parents went to college. Her father was a stern disciplinarian. My father had a gentle voice, and was easy to get along with. Rita's father had a dark, full moustache. I remember trying to see if he ever smiled. Somehow his moustache covered the top lip and he appeared foreboding. Her mother was a considerate person. The most outstanding thing I remember about her was that she had one blue eye and one brown eye. I found this interesting since I had never seen a person with such characteristics. I was too shy to ask or comment about it.

We went to each other's weddings and sent holiday greetings to one another. When I moved to California and occasionally visited New York, I always met her for lunch and we talk about how lucky we were to have shared our childhood years together.

On one of my last visits to New York, I noticed Rita wasn't herself. She seemed quite rigid in her appearance and had difficulty walking. Little did I know until later that same year, she had developed Parkinson's disease. This condition did not slow down our visits or correspondence with one another. Recently, I heard through another friend, that Rita was in a home that cares for people with Alzheimer's disease. I was *devastated* when I heard the terrible news and couldn't believe that this horrible disease could happen to my very first and best childhood friend.

Rita will forever be an important part of my childhood memories.

A Surprising Chapter in My Life

by Lita Askansas

Several years ago, I remember sitting by the kitchen window and looking out. I admired the green leafy trees and beautiful pastel colors.

All of a sudden my eyes turned toward a sturdy looking woman walking her large dog. Somehow her lively steps and constant chatter with her dog brought out an envious recognition for me.

I realized that I would love to take a walk with a dog of my own. The thought of a pull on the leash, giving a command to stop and go, and holding a small dog could bring more joy into my life. These thoughts consumed me the entire day.

That night I quietly approached my husband with the idea of us getting a dog. Our home was relatively quiet and very tidy. It was kind of STILL.

"Wouldn't it be fun at our age to care for and to love a little dog?" I asked Charles. I let him know that I was totally aware of the responsibilities it would take.

We would, of course, have to change certain areas of our lives—such as preparation for traveling. Do we take the dog with us or get a pet sitter? There would be things like, taking the dog for walks and all kinds of training.

Well, I decided for both of us. "Yes," I said, "I definitely think we are ready to undertake the responsibilities." Then I added, "Honey, life is just a bit too uncomplicated. It is time that we messed things up a little."

After several long discussions during a period of two weeks, I made the final decision for both Charles and me.

Thus, Buddy came into our lives. Buddy is a shit zu, very loving, extremely gentle and an absolute joy.

When we go on small trips, Charles and I often like to take him with us. We pack up the car, just like we used to do with our children—we make sure we have Buddy's food, water, plastic bags and of course, his comfortable bed.

During the Christmas holidays, we went to Carmel for three days. We took Buddy with us. There are many places that will allow pets and we are starting to learn the locations of them all.

While walking in Carmel I said to Charles, "Look at the woman across the street, wearing a black and tan pantsuit and a pair of sunglasses. You can see her poking her husband to take a look at Buddy." They both came over and talked to us and to Buddy for ten minutes. They actually asked if they could play with him.

I honestly believe that Buddy is a happy dog, even though at times I would like to know what he is thinking. I hope he has good thoughts and that he feels safe!

Lita Says Good-bye

by Lita Askansas

These are words straight from my heart. I can't thank the memoir writing group enough for the support and love that I have felt through the years.

As time went by during the last several years, my life has changed considerably. I feel that through the words that I have written, a new sense of acceptance for myself has taken place. Even though I have had a substantial and exciting career, I truly never felt that I was gifted in any way.

I realized that "yes," I do have a gift and perhaps it is writing and hopefully it will one day continue for me.

Thank you for helping me gain more confidence in myself. The loss of my husband was so debilitating – not only his death, but the journey through the few years of his illness and his diminished life.

I realize that this class and Louise have helped me get through this difficult time. I must say that I have exited from sadness and entered a world of experiencing happiness and even joy at this time.

Dorothy Atkins

My work is subtle, rhythmic, colorful and poetic. I live my life with purpose as a highly energetic motivational speaker and entrepreneur with a line of greeting cards that once caught the eye of Robert Redford. My life was just beginning after many years in banking. Forecasting and number crunching left little time in my head to really make a serious attempt to do what I had longed to do for years, and that was to paint, write poetry and to do public speaking.

My acrylic and oils are vibrant in color and evoke the memories, wonder, and stories of my childhood and slices of my everyday life. The presence of women, soft, strong, joyful and engaging take center stage in my work.

I am a self-taught artist who maintains humor, rhythm and spirituality in my images, but I contend that art is a definite and continual sense of discovery.

I have exhibited my work at Gallery Saratoga, Bank of America, Guglielmo Winery, Saratoga Community Center, Saratoga Garden Art Show, La Quinta Hotel, MOAD (Museum of African Diaspora) San Francisco, Triton Museum, Los Gatos Jewish Community Center, and Le Petit Trianon Theatre.

My work has also been featured in Charles Schwab magazine and Internet video, Scene Magazine, Victoria magazine, AARP and various newspaper articles.

My paintings are in private collections throughout the world.

I am President of Northern California National League of American Pen Women.

I first met Louise Webb when I joined the National League of American Pen Women in 2006. Over the years she has invited me to join her writing class. She saw something in me that I had wanted to do for years but always put it off. Finally, I took the leap and now feel like I am on my way to accomplish a dream of writing my memoirs.

Contact:
fromwhereisit@sbcglobal.net
www.dorothyatkinsartist.com

Advantage of Simple

by Dorothy Atkins

I recall our youth quite differently than Dean.

He lived right next door.

When closing my eyes I see neat rows of duplexes and grassy knolls.

He told me only yesterday it was government housing,

The Projects.

Sweet memories of the shopping center with ten-cent candy and Double Bubble.

Dean says it was a corner store.

We were not fancy folks.

I remember the tall eucalyptus engulfing a rustic yard.

It was an empty lot surrounded with dirt.

I remember a neat playhouse filled with momentous books and things.

Dean reminded me it was flatten boxes with newspaper floors.

I am certain I fell asleep to the sound of a harp.

The Chief in a drunken stupor.

Certainly those wonderful nights on a marshmallow roast had to be more than families just sharing a sparse meal.

We did agree when it came to love.

His mom crossing the quarantine line when my brother was sick,

Mrs. Cohen giving us midday snacks,

playing on the open cliffs,

running all the way up Tank Hill until we thought we would drop,

sniffing orange poppies in the midday sun,

long nights around the radio sound,

telling secrets and playing pretend.

We both remembered in color.

We were wonderful folks.

Home Bound

by Dorothy Atkins

Hours and hours of airtime, delayed connections and changing planes had begun to take its toll. This was my first North meets South visit to Jackson, Mississippi. My first impression was how tiny the airport was. Not a trip I wanted to make, but my dad wanted to return to his boyhood home after the death of my mom, and I needed some time with him as a Daddy's girl. I suppose I would follow him anywhere. Mississippi is hot humid and very still with spectacular scenery of tall timbers and lush greenery. I closed my eyes trying to take it all in that I was in the Deep South. This place reminded me of Lake Tahoe with pure air and miles and miles of narrow roads. At times we did not pass another car as we continued our journey. A certain feeling of uncertainty was present as I passed the time looking out of the car window. Small town after small town, with names like D Low and Pinole each had a church on its main road. Then, another 45 minutes of travel time.

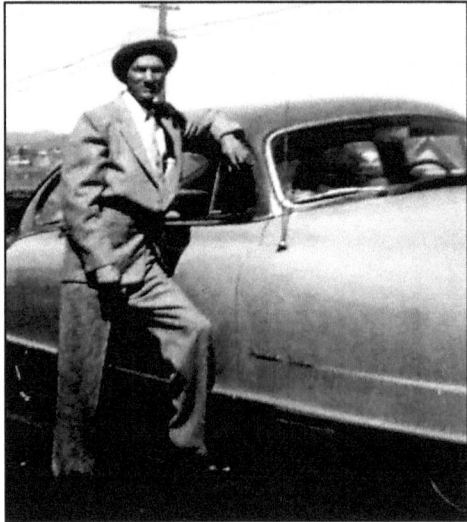

It seems true that country miles are just as far as the crow flies. Once settled in, I sat in total awe of how my daddy told stories of running from the sheriff as a boy in those woods guided only by the shimmering light of the moon. Guns blaring and no doubt coon dogs howling with the scent of a wanted man filling the still night. Of course, the offense was fornicating with someone's wife or moonshine. Or better yet, the effects of both. Imagine no street signs, no visible markers of where you are or even where you are headed. In a moment I knew I would never travel anywhere in these parts after sunset. After all, I had seen the movie Defiant Ones with Sidney Poitier and Tony Curtis years ago.

My daddy had perfect recall of every dirt road running along the Strong River. How could this almost 90 year-old man describe in vivid detail how he and the McIntosh brothers walked for miles in the woody woods in search of wine, women and juke joints. He pointed to a boarded up church showing miles and years of decay that stood in the majestic sunlight, pretty much as it had in his youth. Stories seemed to resound and flow from the planks on the windows. It wasn't hard to listen faintly for my favorite hymn or for the sound of blues in the wind. "WOW!" was a feeling.

Going to the south took on a new meaning as it had, of course, for my daddy. California speaks to me of my formative years, but Mississippi held a mesmerizing power on things I had heard most of my life, filling my soul as though I had just received a new organ donated from the spirits of my kinfolk. How can one be out of sorts with the heady scent of magnolias filling every nook and cranny? At that moment in time, I was overcome.

Years of history and suffering flashed before my weary eyes then suddenly we approached a small bridge in an area much like the willowing Redwoods. I am sad to say that urban graffiti had not escaped the countryside. In bold red lettering it read KKK Reigns. My daddy sensing my sudden discomfort and silence spoke in a softening low voice sending chills to my weary legs and bones.

"My rifle in the gun rack is loaded and so is my handgun."

"Guns, guns, guns," I thought. "Where am I?" More thoughts popped in my head, imagination overpowering any sense of realism. What must run-away slaves, or any person of color, experienced as they fled through these plush backwoods in total darkness? How could some place so beautiful, lovely and seemingly pure hold so many daunting memories? Suddenly, I replied to my daddy's statement. "Sure, loaded guns," I said barely above a whisper.

At last, we arrived in Shivers. I noticed to my right a somewhat modern sign announcing the town name. One gets the real sense that time has stood still.

Big Cat Little Cat

by Dorothy Atkins

Excerpts from my travel journey.
Always with my box of 64-crayola crayons.

Opening my drapes this morning, I noticed the neighbor's cat basking in the sun. In the past, my opinion about cats was deep in Cat Lore surrounded around legends and much superstition. Although I have echoed out loud more than once that I did not like cats, my opinion has changed forever after a planned trip to New York.

Upon arriving at the home of a dear friend that I had not seen in over twenty years, she inquired very casually, "Are you allergic to cats?" "Don't think so," was my casual reply. My interest in cats before then had not been more than National Geographic and watching them from my front window. Since I found them rather mysterious and at times creepy, I had no longing to spend time with them or have them touch me. I was soon to learn that she had three cats that I would spend the next four days with. The first few hours I spent keeping an eye on each cat as they sized me up from a distance. Unlike dogs, they did not come barking, wagging their tails or trying to lick all over me. They merely walked around deciding how they felt and if they would allow me to come near them. It was very clear within minutes the three of them had full run of the place and were in charge without uttering a sound. No doubt their Egyptian Royalty had survived since Cleopatra.

After a while, their synchronized moves turned into a rather laid back don't give a darn attitude. Home free! I thought, "They won't bother me, I won't bother them." Little did I know, cats decide when they will allow you into their space, not the other way around. For most of the day, they slept in their favorite spots and ignored my comings and goings. Naps have a way of rejuvenating me and it works the same with cats. Suppose it has something to do with domesticating them from that larger cat, the lion, whose days are spent napping only to roar at night. Nocturnal you know.

By nightfall, I felt the effects of my long flight and was eager to find my bed on the sofa. Within moments, I had drifted off into a very sound sleep. What seemed like hours later, and startled by the sound of paws hitting the hardwood, I gasped in fright. Piercing little eyes that shown like fireflies darting back and forth scared me fully awake. Three cats in precise harmony leaped and sang to the quietness of the night. Sleep by now was a distant thought as my superstitions and Cat Lore raced through my head. Surely I would be attacked during the night. But what I found to be true, cats decide when they will allow you into their world. Each cat used my body for the remainder of the night to leap from one favorite spot to another, playing cat tag. After all, I had entered their space and their

royal bloodline would not allow them to give it up until they choose to surrender. Unable to watch the darting eyes any longer, I drifted to sleep only to awaken the next morning to find three cats snuggled on my chest fast asleep. Cats make strange

bedfellows and sleeping with three is one pussy too many.

Mabel Brix

I am ninety-seven years old and have been a member of Louise's Memoir Class for a long time. I first met Louise when I attended her class after a visit to the Saratoga Senior Center. I saw the class was being offered and decided to give it a try. That was about twelve years ago.

I especially enjoyed the male members: Max and Jim who could always make me laugh.

I have written many stories and put them in a notebook with pictures for my grandchildren. Many of my stories tell about my Danish heritage and my employment at I Magnin Company. Even today I think of stories I should write as I compare present day Oakland with the Oakland of my childhood. In class, I remember Louise's hats as she also likes to dress tastefully.

Mabel Brix
In Loving Memory
1918 - 2016

Mother's Day, 2015

by Mabel Brix

**In memory of my own mother
and all the wonderful things she taught me.**

My mother, Elsie Marie Pauline Winther Sorensen, often quoted this saying:

> "What we call luck
> Is simply pluck
> And doing things over and over.
> Courage and will,
> Perseverance and skill,
> Are the four leaves of luck's clover."

I HAD A GREAT MOM

She was the most powerful, important person in my life. I am grateful to her, a woman of insight, who always gave me advice about life, giving and loving, forgiveness, trust and kindness and being the best I could be.

I have always endeavored to be like my mom.

Having a loving mother and thoughtful one who demonstrates the meaning of love tells me that my mom was a truly thoughtful, loving, and giving woman.

Through self-sacrifice and actual giving of herself, I had instruction in voice, all dance classes including ballet, interpretive, and tap lessons, hair appointments and even a new sweater. She cleaned homes in exchange. No money was given. All was accomplished through bartering. Her love had the greatest impression on me.

Her love was the greatest gift to me. Her demonstration to me was so perfect!

This day there are so many things I am thankful for, like waking to a new day with a fresh start each morning, noon and nighttime too.

I am grateful for good health and pray that family and friends will be well. I am very grateful for a loving family and the feeling of belonging and having had the love of a special man, my husband for 47 years, whom I feel is still with me.

I have loved being a daughter, sister, wife, mother, mother-in-law, grandmother and great grandmother, and to have experienced the birth of my three sons who I love and adore.

I am grateful for the miracle of sight, so I can take in the beauty and color of nature, the trees, flowers, hills, and mountains. And watching our dog Millie during our walks on the beautiful beach at the Sea Ranch where the surf is so rough and powerful.

I have enjoyed the sounds of light and lovely music, grand, powerful symphonies, the bagpipes that make me smile and cry, and the voices of loved ones.

I have enjoyed the companionship of my Mahjong pals and our visits across the United States. We love each other and our families. After 50 years we are still talking with each other—what a gift. I am so grateful to have friends that have been close through all conditions, the love and warmth, the laughter, the meals. They will always be part of my extended family, as will my Danish Lodge sisters, how lucky can you be?

"Is it luck or just pluck?"

Is it pre-ordained or does it come from our own desires?

I am so grateful for the pleasure of finding fabulous, cozy talented, smart people to spend the time with, sharing life and experiences. So far, I feel lucky like the four leaves of luck's clover. We all have it—courage, will, perseverance and skill.

"Spoon Fashion"
NEW YORK, NEW YORK—HERE I COME!

by Mabel Brix

In 1942 all train travel was solidly booked with business people and military personnel, all feeling very lucky and fortunate to have a ticket—all loving the clickety clack of the train, as we sped across the countryside.

Preparation for a buying trip called for countless hours taking inventory submitting budgets, making appointments with old and new manufactures and telling management about plans and intention for the coming months and then asking for the funding needed to floor the hopefully profitable next season of business. I had great expectations!

Considering all the busy work one of our secretaries made—all hotel accommodations and travel accommodations—did we get our usual roomette or bedroom? NO! She put another buyer and me in the same berth—very cozy!

Well, there were no accommodations – oh well, this was not the Orient Express. We couldn't kill the secretary (she was a nice lady). We sighed a lot and said a lot of "Oh Wells." We were young, good friends, both newlyweds, oh, well, we would make the best of it.

The first night out we laughed about our situation and other things and how men go to bed but women have "to get ready for bed." Of course, this is why there is a need for lingerie buyers like me—you have to look good—you cannot "just go to bed."

So, Jan was off to the lounge for the "get ready" part of going to bed. I was next—going to the lounge was fine the light was on. However, when I had finished and opened the lounge door, the overhead light had been lowered and it was difficult to distinguish where one berth ended and another began. I counted one, two, three, four—this is the one.

As I jumped into the berth I said, "Oh, Boy, it is really cold tonight, we have to sleep spoon fashion to keep warm."

For a moment there was silence, then out of the darkness a very deep voice said, "That sounds very interesting!"

I removed myself faster than an Olympic track star. I found Jan, giggled a bit and started to speculate about the poor man and what he thought of the idiot that jumped into his birth, "Oh, dear—what now?"

The next morning we hesitantly headed for the dining car. Would he be there? Would we see an angry person? Such tension. But we forged ahead, God forbid we go without breakfast. We did our best to be formal, serious and dignified.

We were seated and I made a great effort not to look around. All that was lost when something caught my eye. There he was—a handsome gentleman looking as though he was waiting for us. He smiled, lifted his spoon and waved it back and forth over his shoulder! With that, he rose and left the dining car.

When I returned to California, my husband Harry teased me about the "Berth Incident" and had great fun starting a lovely serving spoon collection for me. To this day, when I see a special spoon, I buy it.

I think my embarrassing moment turned out great! A silly, stupid moment in my life that I will never forget!

Grace Bush

I was born in Cambridge, Massachusetts in 1939 and lived there for 31 years. I met my husband at Cambridge High and Latin School. This August we celebrated our 55th wedding anniversary. Thirty-three years ago we settled in Saratoga. We have four children and four grandchildren, one of whom just graduated cum laude from San Francisco State and another who is the star of her kindergarten class in Reno, Nevada.

After retiring, I joined the Saratoga Senior Center. I went to a class to freshen my bridge skills. I met Charlotte Vukelich at the bridge group and one day memoir writing came up. Charlotte told me about this writing class and showed me an example of a memoir. I was hooked and brought myself to the Senior Center in early 2013. I met Louise at the class and at each meeting I received some good information, hints and advice from her.

I've wanted to write my memoirs for a long time – to tell about the people in my life who influenced me. Hopefully these stories will help others to find special moments in their life.

Recently, with the reading of some of our personal memoirs, the word therapy came up to describe us. How true! It is comforting to know you can read a memoir that is close to your heart and be understood. Nothing we experience is a 'first.' Praise and suggestions are helpful to express the emotion in your heart.

In my first meeting, I heard Loraine tell one of her stories set in Chico. I learned she did that often. It made me think of my Point Shirley, Winthrop, Massachusetts stories. Jim's memoirs sounded a lot like some of my husband's stories. I could see it from 'outside' the loop.

We gain understanding of each other by sharing our stories with seriousness and kindness. My favorite laugh, was after I read my memoir about my mother. More than a few cried, "THAT SOUNDS LIKE MY MOTHER!"

Who Am I?

by Grace Bush

Over the past few months I have come to clarify what I want to do with my writing. Hearing others explain what they are doing, want to do, try to do has helped a lot. Also going through the memorabilia of my mother and the rest of her family, I have become grateful to see them in new ways. My sister has become involved in ancestry.com so is filling me in on things I did not know or had little inklings about. That firmed for me – what I should do – so to start......

I know who I am – Grace Elizabeth Crockett Jr. from 72 ½ Inman Street, Cambridge, Massachusetts 02139 and that '72 ½' has made me special.

Even today, it is not unusual to be called 'Grace Jr.' when visiting back in Massachusetts. How many times do you think I had to explain that '1/2'? Do you know of anyone else who lives in '1/2' addressed house? 72 ½ was one of three houses on the property – also 72 and 72A. 72 was built shortly after the Civil War by my great grandfather. 72 ½ was connected to 72 to accommodate the large family back then but walled off to become a rental property. 72A became my grandparents' home in the 50s.

Now get this: At age 28 I moved to 72 Inman Street – yup, I had finally made it and given the intervening years you would know how and why I made it.

This is not a 'climb all over others' story to reach this 'phase in life'. This story is about the people in my life who influenced me, who provided good examples and who taught me about life by their life decisions and behaviors. They showed me what being 'special' meant.

Inman Street was in a middle class neighborhood then – as that applied in the 1940s and 1950s in Cambridge, Massachusetts. The world was moving out of depression and into war. Folks were hanging on. The tenants at 72 Inman Street at the time had a son being held as a POW in the Pacific theater of the war. The Fennell family at 77 Inman Street saw their father away from home for days as a long haul truck driver, but he had a job. The Olesens, Burns, Colemans and Solomons were all hard working families making it during tough times and building a true neighborhood family. It was diverse before most of us could define or spell diverse with Italians, Greeks, Portuguese and African-Americans living with Irish and English folks.

I hope these stories will show the wonderful people, places and events that have brought me to this writing group. (** thanks to Charlotte Vukelich **)

Finding my way
To the end of the path,
Thankful to those
Who pointed to the prize,
All along much help,
All along lots of trips and falls.
In the words of my children
Are we there yet Mom?

"MA"

by Grace Bush

Let me introduce Mrs. Grace Elizabeth Crockett, my mother. I was (and still am) Grace Elizabeth Crockett, Jr. That pretty much says it all. I was Grace, Jr. to all, but few relatives are still alive to remember. That is why sisters are important. Mine could not say Grace, Jr. when she came along and shortened my name to Junie. Now, that is the name younger cousins as well as nieces, nephews and in-laws call me.

Grace Elizabeth
Crockett, Sr.

But my original point was that I was designed to be a carbon copy of my mother, so do I really need to write a memoir? I jest.

My mother – what a role model! What a nag! What an advisor! What a ruler! These were my thoughts when I was a young girl. I learned and learned and modeled my life as told – but was never quite right. I was never entirely wrong either. Mother loved me dearly and stood by me in good times and in my seriously down times. What an example to follow.

She cared for her brother, Frank, most of his life. She looked after her parents as they aged, her sister in her pregnancies and her husband and family. Along with that she worked from high school on until I entered the scene. She was a seamstress at one of Boston's fine dress shops. (YAY, got my prom gowns there). She burnished

56

her welder skills during the war at the Watertown Arsenal. She managed my grandfather's rental properties in Cambridge and did some of the painting and wallpapering on the houses as well. Believe me, she shared these skills with this grateful daughter.

After my dad and Frank died – within six weeks of each other, she went back to work as a secretary at the local estate auction house, WF Hubleys. The position enabled her to get the best deals on fantastic furniture and I still eat dinner on a rock maple table that has passed the test of time and shines as brightly as when it was first built.

Mother retired at age 75, sold her house and moved permanently to Point Shirley, Winthrop, Massachusetts – that cottage where so much happiness occurred. In 1998 on the day after Easter, I flew back and picked her up at a hospital and brought her to California – she was 85 then. She was at my home about two weeks when I found her on the bathroom floor after a stroke. She survived

Grace with her mother, Grace, at Point Shirley

another eight years after many hospital and rehab stays and finally in the board and care of Lina Wang, my guiding angel. My daughter provided hospice care and I was able to be with my mother when she passed.

To sum up, her goodness won me over but I still had to put up with some *&^&^^%' during my life.

Her focus was on rules, and they were strict. I had a list of household duties from easy at six years old to complex at 16. I was given advice on all possible events that could take place and was rarely surprised as she knew everything. Mother was an avid church worker, active in all kinds of money raising activities and was a part of a group of women with children like me. Hence, they chatted and knew all the goings on of our age group.

One afternoon I went to confession and took a friend with me – yes, right into the confessional. This friend was younger than I, eight years old, and I thought she should be aware of what was ahead for her. Mother's friends, of course, dropped by on the way home from church to alert her. I was then laid on mother's lap and given my one and only spanking. I didn't receive another punishment until the truancy was revealed, so her sermons on proper behavior kept me in line.

As I got older, finished college and started teaching school, I began to see the wisdom of mother's ways as she faced her struggles with life, including her brother's death, my sister's birth and having a nervous breakdown. In 1960 she was hospitalized. Then I showed up with Chuck and announced to her and my dad our engagement. Her planning for such an affair as our wedding, helped her get better fast. Mother informed me of all things that could go wrong in a marriage – heck Chuck didn't even have a job. "No, Ma, he was a Lieutenant (junior grade), in the US Navy, deployed to Cuba to keep the Russians out of our neighborhood." My father's affection for Chuck won her over and I did raise my champagne glass to her on my 50th wedding anniversary.

Of course, advice on raising my own children was plentiful, and by this time we lived in the house at 72 Inman St. No more 72 ½ for me. Mother lived in 72A, but she didn't comment on my loud voice in admonishing my four children.

By this time I was gaining the experience that she had – I could see the value of all she tried to teach me. Not to say she wasn't still advising. More of her comments were now to improve Chuck which may have made the attraction to move away more exciting.

Mother's travels to visit us in Oklahoma and California gave her some adventure and tales to tell her coworkers at Hubleys.

When my sister moved to California and married, she would come for a month, spending two weeks at each house. I was glad my sister got to experience mother's wisdom on marriage and Chuck was happy that my sister's husband became the focus of her marital criticism.

She was a wonderful Nana and her seven grandchildren gave her an audience for her wisdom. She is remembered for haircuts that were proper, being a great card player, buying fantastic desserts and adding financial gifts to their birthday parties. Also included was advice on length of skirts, tasteless t-shirts and how old you should be to wear lipstick.

Granny

by Grace Bush

Early insights and experiences during difficult times certainly influence behavior throughout a lifetime. Growing up during war time when my Dad served as a medic in Italy and Mom worked at the local arsenal, left me in the care of my grandparents and Uncle Frank.

My most vivid memory of my grandmother was in early 1944. I was recovering from pneumonia and losing all my hair. I recall sitting on her lap and looking out the window watching my mother walk my dad to the bus stop as he left for Fort Devins and basic training. Granny's project was to restore my health and that she did. Asparagus soup and chocolate ice cream brought success in a short time. Alas, the hair has remained straight ever since!

Life became a series of lessons, most of which I still practice today. I know how to make a lemon meringue pie, stuffing for a roast chicken, coleslaw dressing from scratch, clean a kitchen, do laundry, play a game of bridge, iron linen tablecloths and clean silver. I called it fun then.

It was two years of vivid memories – air raids at night, blackout curtains for houses, early bedtimes since lights out was early in the fall. In those days there was no chewing gum sold at the candy store. We learned math skills at school and even more at home playing cards. I have many memories of afternoons in the pantry helping Granny with dinner plans. Before the war ended, my grandparents celebrated their 50th anniversary. Their children all took their ration cards and chipped in to give them 50 pounds of sugar! They'd be drinking sugar in their tea for years! My time there only lasted two years, but my relationship with Granny lasted 24 years in total.

Our friendship grew after I returned to my home in Cambridge. Granny had to take a bus and a train to Boston to meet my mother and on my birthdays we would celebrate with lobster dinners at Steuben's restaurant. She and mother would each have a martini to start and I would get the two olives. I have maintained my love of lobster all these 75 plus years, but only had a martini after age 60.

My grandparents moved back to Cambridge in the 1950s and shortly thereafter celebrated their 60th anniversary. From grammar school through high school and college I'd drop in daily to visit and chat with them all. Grandpa was retired now and loved the visits. Frank would be home from school too for a card game or some help with trigonometry! Granny would make us all a cup of tea.

I was able to return all the favors she had done for me by doing her errands and weekly house chores while I was in high school and college. She rewarded me and those earnings enabled me to pay for my carfare and lunches while in college.

My grandmother was most loved by her husband. After her passing, in going through her belongings we found love notes he had written and the gifts he had given her. Granny had seven children and 18 other grandchildren over the years and was loved by all. In her final years her children and grandchildren were always dropping by, fixing things around the house and doing errands for her. She was a loved woman. Grandmother passed away in February of 1963 a few days before her 86th birthday.

I have carried on and taught my children these lessons and there is rarely a party without a lemon meringue pie. This month I will take my granddaughter on our 19th or 20th birthday dinner to celebrate her 21st birthday – at Boston Billy's Chowder House in Los Gatos, the closest I have found yet for good lobster.

Uncle Frank

by Grace Bush

Uncle Frank was my godfather, my best friend as a child, my mentor as a teen and my political confidant as a young adult. Frank Asaph Gilbert has had quite an influence on my life and on who I am today. It is not easy to list all the ways in which he influenced my life.

Frank was the second child in a family of seven, born in 1900. He had four brothers and two sisters, my mother was the youngest girl. All the children grew up in Cambridge, Massachusetts in a house my great grandfather had built soon after the Civil War. As he entered the teen years, he developed what was then known as 'infantile paralysis'. My grandmother sought help for him tirelessly in what was and is still known as one of the finest medical areas in the country. There was not much known then about what turned out to be polio in the 1950s.

Frank's disease was not threatening, however he had to learn to write with his left hand and adjust to a much weakened left leg. Undaunted, Frank attended Cambridge High and Latin School and earned his B.A. in Mathematics at Boston College. Though stymied physically, he went on to teach mathematics at Boston Latin School for 40 years. He lived with his parents the rest of their life and with my parents after his parents died.

In 1929 the family moved to Watertown, Massachusetts and rented the Cambridge property which by now had three houses on it, 72, 72 ½, 72A. During his teaching years in Watertown, he bought a car and had a colleague keep the car and drive him to school every day. In the 1950s the family moved back to Cambridge into their property at 72A, right next to our house, 72 ½. My grandparents were elderly now, my grandfather retired and my mother was able to tend to their needs. Frank sold the car to my father and used a taxi service for the commute to school. By 1956 I was ready to attend Emmanuel College which was on a street adjacent to Boston Latin, so I had built in transportation - well anytime I wanted the 7:00 am ride.

In 1944, at age five, my father headed off to war and I moved to Watertown with my grandparents and Frank as I recovered from pneumonia and ear abscess. Soon after the move, my father left for boot camp in Massachusetts and mountain training in Colorado. My mother found work at the Watertown arsenal as a welder. I had my own Rosie the Riveter to brag about.

Frank became my best friend. The first thing I recall about him was his ear to the radio, listening to the war news. He spent late afternoons reading to me before blackouts necessitated LIGHTS OUT. On weekends he would engage me in card games where I got my first lessons with numbers, a foreshadowing of my future. Slap the Jack, War and then Rummy became favorite games of mine. I was his star pupil on the home front, but not the only one. Cousins would line up on weekends for math tutoring.

We used to see him weekly after the war for Sunday dinners. During the summers we all had cottages at Point Shirley, Winthrop, Massachusetts on the Boston Harbor. We kept up card games, reading and politics (I even remember when President Truman fired General MacArthur).

When I was nine, I insisted that I was old enough to have a bicycle. My parents did not agree. But Frank convinced them that I was both old and able enough to have a bicycle if I rode it only in Winthrop (vs the city of Cambridge). Every young girl should have such a champion.

With his counsel and help in high school, I did well in mathematics and ended up with math as my major in college. Frank was able to inspire me, to give me confidence in my abilities, and along with my dad, convince me I could be SOMETHING.

During those years we challenged ourselves on crossword puzzles. Frank, however, got the Sunday paper with the big puzzle of the week. Aha, as soon as I got a job, I got one of those puzzles (and still do).

He turned me on to his favorite mystery writers – Agatha Christie and Rex Stout. His library was a super source for my reading.

Frank became a painter and a cartoonist. Those cartoons still live on in an envelope my mother saved. Any EVENT in our family was put into a cartoon by Frank.

By 1963 my grandparents had died so my parents moved in to live with Frank and I got to return to my childhood home with my family at 72 ½ Inman St. For the next few years Frank became their reader and card teacher.

Frank died in March of 1966, two months after my dad passed away.

They were the men in my life who inspired me and told me what I could do with my life. They encouraged me to never settle for less.

Ellie

by Grace Bush

One of the folks I mentioned in my last memoir is my longest friend, Ellie. From earliest days in the 50s, she has encouraged me to write. Then, it was just the curious, weird jokes I'd write to her over the winters. Since then she has encouraged me to write and capture our fun times, both good and bad. She started reminding me again when we hooked up again at age 50, and has been my best audience.

I met Ellie Cafferty in 1943 after we both turned four years old. We met in Point Shirley, Winthrop, Massachusetts during the Second World War and remained friends for the many summers we vacationed in this beach community. Point Shirley was a peninsula of Winthrop, stretching out with the Atlantic Ocean

Grace and Ellie

on one side and Boston Harbor on the other side. Point Shirley was a small community in those days, mostly summer people for many years and a safe place for young kids to play and learn and develop strong friendships. It was safe enough for us to have bicycles and we rode over the entire area – from the sea wall to the sandy beach on the Atlantic Ocean side to the Deer Island prison on the tip as well as the Water Tower at the head. This wonderful town has been written about by Sylvia Plath in her poem, Point Shirley, part of her book The Colossus and Other Poems.

Along the harbor side, a sea wall separated the water from the street – Grand View Avenue. The grand view was of Logan Airport and more importantly the Boston skyline. The colonial era Custom House could be seen before the famous John Hancock super tower was built. The airport changed about as much as Ellie and I did over the next 15 years. We can safely say we never got as loud as its new jet planes despite some grand spectacular parties we hosted over that time.

When we met at four years old we were both living in the same rental duplex cottage. I was an only child at the time, but Ellie had a sister and two brothers, one of whom, Kevin, became part of our triumvirate. Days were spent climbing over the seawall – which was just a short walk down Deepwater Street. We would hunt for crabs by turning over the rocks. Periwinkles were easier to find, and clams were a bit too clever for us to unearth. We never touched the plentiful mussels – but then Boston Harbor was not known for its pure clean water in those days. My mother was noted for retrieving a periwinkle from Kevin's nose with one of her crochet hooks. She was our swimming teacher and lifeguard as we familiarized ourselves with this beach.

Weekends were spent with extended family, all pitching in with ration cards for picnics on the shared front porch. Ellie's parents were from Ireland and there were plenty of aunts, uncles and cousins. Ellie's dad ran a butcher shop in the famous Boston Haymarket so we sometimes had lamb chops. At least I fell in love with them then! My dad worked at a magazine distributing company and his donations were comic books which the five of us scoffed up. But not for long as he left for the war in Italy in early 1944.

Each July 4th, everyone on the Point got together to march in the "horrible parade" after which they gathered for a series of games and contests. Afternoons were for young children to decorate their bicycles, tricycles and doll carriages and parade around the church center. Evenings were for teenagers and adults dancing in the same center.

We spent weekdays at the playground where we learned all the new games, played cards, softball and whatever else was popular at the time. It is only now that I recognize how special those summers were – ten weeks of great weather, learning and hilarious fun. Ellie and I realize today how lucky we were to have those small town vacations away from the big cities we lived in during winters. "For Yoga lovers, when asked to put yourself in a happy, calm place, I choose that sea wall and the slurping waves."

Ellie and I continued our summer friendship – a friendship over the years. Two girls who shared their first period and first boyfriends, now share their 'loose bowels' and assorted ailments. But boy didn't it all start with the great joke that had them wetting their pants. A bit of foreshadowing I can say today. Alas, I only remember the 'big' picture punch line and not too much about the rest of the story. As we sat in the back of my father's 1947 Dodge, someone told this story:

"Mom mistakenly sprinkled Ex-Lax over the ice cream. Later in the evening she asked Dad how he liked the dessert. His reply 'cemented' the friendship. "It was great but when I bent over to feed the cat, I shot the dog".

We ended up rolling on the floor of the car and tears of laughter were falling. More jokes surfaced over the years often instigated by number three in our gang, Kevin.

Kevin was a year younger than Ellie but he had LOTS of friends that helped us build our confidence in dealing with MEN – well, boys. Oh, I wish that last hurricane in 1970 had not soaked all my teen diaries!!

All the 'firsts' in my life were done with Ellie – our first bike ride, our first row boat trip, our first roller coaster ride, our first bus ride, our first cigarette, our first drink, our first jobs at the bank, our first sharings with trust, our first secrets – all shared at Point Shirley. Each first is worthy of its own memoir.

Again, as the ages increased, we became more daring in our adventures. We played about every board and card game known at the time. We were adept swimmers and divers. Canasta was fun, but renting a boat and rowing to Snake Island was courageous and it allowed us to smoke without ever getting caught! Other days we would get on bikes and pedal to Revere Beach for a ride on the famous Cyclone roller coaster. The summer after we entered high school we implored Kevin to invite his friends to play cards with us and attend our beach parties, both day and night. Girls meet boys. Delightful! These freedoms gave us the spirit of independence.

The teen years were spent busing to Boston to work at the city banks followed by weekend dances at the local yacht club. We'd usually meet each evening with our group of six or seven friends at the local clam shack, occasionally getting together for pajama parties.

Of course, with the late teen years we were working for the summer in preparation for attending college and becoming responsible members of society. Life had become more serious and now Chuck was in my life.

Despite some separations due to military service, work experiences and moves from the area, Ellie and I have remained friends. We kept in touch via email and Point Shirley friends and I know the years of childhood, peppered with Point Shirley's activities have bonded us forever. We both raised families and moved about, suffered some family losses but reunited in San Francisco to

Grace and Ellie

celebrate our 50th birthdays. We spent the weekend laughing over
our childhood thrills and catching up and have been in touch ever
since. We met at the Ritz Carlton in Dana Point for our 70th
birthday and, God willing, the Winthrop Yacht Club or Wegener's
clam shack for number 75.

My First Boy-Friend(s)

by Grace Bush

This subject gave me pause – allowing time to recall and remember the pleasure of those meetings and friendships. First boyfriend would be really determined by definition of boy hyphen friend or one word, boyfriend.

In Miss Wadden's third grade class, Roland Manning was my friend, but also a partner in crime. We learned how to stand in the corner together, which gave us time to really know each other. Fourth and fifth grade brought Tommy Coady and Richie Sullivan into my life and into many fun activities (during) and after school on the days we were dismissed from school in time for an adventure.

But then I emailed with Ellie, friend from my summer vacation days and whose brother was a provider of many boy friends with whom we could plan summer adventures. Dave McLaughlin and Bobby Farrell spent the summers of fifth and sixth grade on the beach with us a few days a week. Other days we played baseball or checkers over at the park. You may recall the many card games that were popular then (Canasta and Whist come to mind) so of course we had teams and challenges that sometimes ran late into the dark while we sat on blankets at the beach listening to the waves break on shore. The only snag in these friendships was that they were summer deals. Ellie and I started our many phone conservations over the winter in which she promoted my writing stories of our summers. We had not discovered using buses and streetcars to meet in Boston during the winter until we got into our teens.

1953 came along and so did high school. It was then I met Chuck Bush who became a winter 'friend'. Chuck was not interested in taking the two buses and two trains to visit me in summer so I hung out with what was available and they were great BOY-FRIENDS.

Summer that year brought new friends like Kevin into my life as well as Steve and Bill. I cannot remember their last names but dances at the yacht club and afternoons on the beach suggested we were growing up beyond card game friendships.

To conclude, there were lots of boy-friends, but Chuck was (and still is) my first BOYFRIEND.

Teaching school, raising four children, two girls and two boys, and giving customers tech support for many years also provided many men friends as well as women friends, some of whom will show up in a future memoir.

The Gin Game

by Grace Bush

A short story about a long friendship

This long friendship began in 1959 at the United States Navy, Officer Candidate School in Newport, Rhode Island. My husband, Chuck, became friends with Norman Hall while they trained for their four years of service on the aircraft carrier, the USS Lake Champlain.

Many vignettes abound during the Navy years and are repeatedly told and enhanced during the many reunions we have had over the following years. We first got together in our homes of New York City and Cambridge, Massachusetts followed by more frequent get-togethers when we all ended up on either side of San Francisco, California.

It was the GIN GAME that bonded us whether in Novato or Saratoga. For thirty years we met for a good dinner followed by a gin game. Whether we met at the newest 'hot' restaurant, for someone's milestone birthday, at family weddings, or at one of Norman and Shirley's theater performances, we could always find the time for a game of cards.

Sometimes we would propose meeting beyond Novato or Saratoga. Over the years we have played gin rummy in Vancouver, BC, Seattle, Washington, Houston, Texas, Natchez, Massachusetts and New Orleans, Louisiana. However, our favorite spot was Sea Ranch in Sonoma County. Walks on the beach, fantastic home cooked meals and the perennial gin game made for great weekends.

As you might perceive from the repetition of 'good meals', a common love was fine dining – whether at our homes or one of many fantastic restaurants in the Bay Area.

In 1988 in a visit to number three Navy buddy, in Massachusetts, we stopped in New Orleans to test the many wonderful stories we'd heard about Cajun cuisine. Commander's Palace and Cochon were two of my favorites for dinner after beignet breakfasts and oyster lunches. This first visit to New Orleans found us at the Bombay Club where we were introduced to the pre-dinner martini, hence the sub-comment of this memoir.

To cap this story and tie all the thoughts and ideas together, in 2008 Norman and Shirley were cast in the play, 'THE GIN GAME', played on Broadway by the married couple, Hume Cronyn and Jessica Tandy. Chuck and I took our grandchildren to the performance. Our teens were most impressed with this portrayal of folks in the retirement home playing gin rummy. My daughter commented, "Is this your future, Mom and Dad?" They were even more impressed when I shared some of the emotions of our REAL gin games.

To that end I may add, the three grandchildren are now good gin players. Only last weekend I was chef in Saratoga and Shirley and I were the winners of the GIN GAME. I think age is shining nicely on me. Chuck and Norman were using their math skills to determine just how long this friendship has lasted and maybe we need to visit New Orleans again.

Loraine Barkham Campbell

I started writing stories when I was in the sixth or seventh grade, maybe even earlier, and have been writing ever since. It wasn't until I started attending Louise Webb's class that I started writing my memoirs.

I first met Louise at a Newcomer's Club in Saratoga. We had lived in Saratoga years before but had moved away in 1988. We moved back in 1995 and that's when I joined the Newcomer's Club. She announced to our club that she was leading a memoirs class and invited us to attend.

My granddaughter asked me a question which made me think of my life while living in Chico and it brought back many memories. I now had much to write about Chico and my many adventures and boyfriends while living there.

My husband has passed away but we were married for 66 years. We have three children, three grandchildren, and six greatgrandchildren.

My fond memories of Louise's class is mainly the way we became a family and also Jim teasing me about Chico. I wrote a story about my Chico school and it was chosen for the paper. Jim said, "Let's give her a standing ovation."

> Loraine Barkham Campbell
> In Loving Memory
> 1920 - 2016

Aunt Belle and Loraine Go to the Circus

by Loraine Barkham Campbell

The day promises to be a real scorcher, Sacramento Valley towns don't get much relief from the heat until mid-October. They call this season: Indian summer. Today, September 25, 1925 was certainly no exception.

On East Ninth Street, a little five-year old girl was just waking up. You could catch a glimpse of light red hair and one blue eye peeking over the covers. Loraine loved to be snuggled down in her three quarter sized bed and truly hated to get up in the morning. The small bungalow where she lived with her mother, Alice and her dad, Byron, only had one bedroom. That room was a dressing room for the whole family. It was chopped up by doors: one into the living room, one leading to the bathroom and two more were closets. These openings, along with three dressers didn't leave any room for even a tiny bed for the child.

Almost every house in Chico had a back porch of some kind and this one was screened on three sides. In the winter, they covered the screens with protective canvas. That still didn't keep it from being nippy, when the temperature was in the 30's. Alice, Byron and Loraine slept there year round. When it was really freezing, Byron would wrap a small baby blanket around his head to keep warm. This memory always made Loraine smile.

Just as the little redhead was thinking of going back to sleep, Alice opened the kitchen door and walked onto the porch. She stood by the bed, took hold of the blanket and uncovered Loraine's face. "Wake up, wake up. We have important things to do today."

The girl was rather intrigued by the statement and sat up in bed to learn more. "What are we going to do, Mother?"

"Aunt Belle has a little surprise for you. Now let's get you dressed and I will walk with you to her house."

Aunt Belle and Uncle Bert lived on the corner, two houses away, but the short walk gave Loraine time to think about what her mother had said.

Maybe she was only going to have breakfast with her aunt. But mother said it was a surprise. Maybe Aunt Belle was going to take her someplace. They wouldn't be going far as her aunt didn't drive a car, and the children had never seen her walk more than three blocks.

"Guess, I'll just have to wait and see."

Aunt Belle gave the girl a choice for breakfast. Loraine quickly decided on her favorite-a slice of orange, two pieces of toast, and a cup of coffee with some heavy cream in it—not all melty.

Alice went on her way and left them alone in the kitchen. As they were sipping coffee, Aunt Belle finally said it. "What do you think about the two of use going to the circus this afternoon?" Loraine just couldn't believe her. So this was the surprise! Her face was beaming as she hugged her aunt.

"Can we go right now?"

"No, not until a little later."

The morning dragged on, but finally one o'clock arrived and they could leave the house. Getting to the circus was no problem as the tents were all set up on the corner of Ninth and Pine Streets. Grandma and Grandpa lived at the other end of this same block and the circus was right across the street from them. In fact, Grandpa Buck Barkham always went down to the railroad station on West Fifth with his yellow dray and helped haul circus equipment across town to the vacant lot. Loraine was never allowed to go over there and watch them put up the tents, but she could watch from afar. It was all very exciting.

When the two of them arrived for the afternoon's entertainment, Aunt Belle presented her two passes and they walked inside the tent. The smells, sights, and sounds were overwhelming! They quickly chose seats on a lower level as Aunt Belle was a large woman and climbing the stairs was not for her. It wasn't long before the bright lights went on, spotlighting the circus parade. Loraine loved to watch the acrobats and high wire performance even though it scared her to death. She was afraid of the wild animals and took hold of Aunt Belle's hand for security.

Somewhere in the parade line-up were dwarves. They were really called dwarves in those days. Loraine didn't particularly like to watch these little people and never laughed when they performed. She felt sorry for them as they were constantly running around on their short legs. It must have been painful. Today they were pushing a baby carriage and tossing a doll back and forth. The dwarves always caught the little baby, but somehow it didn't seem very funny. She was glad when the performance was over.

This had been a wonderful day and she thanked Aunt Belle many times. In the late afternoon they started home. After they crossed Pine Street, her aunt paused, leaned over and quietly said, "Wouldn't it be funny if we had a little baby when we got home?" What if the circus dropped one off? You saw the baby they were tossing around, maybe they were trying to find it a new mother and father."

This put a new and exciting thought in Loraine's had, and they both walked faster. No lights were on in Grandma's house or in Alice and Byron's house. They went next door to Aunt Louis and Uncle Bill's home. Alice threw open the front door when she saw them coming. She was standing there holding a real, live breathing baby in her arms. Loraine couldn't believe what she saw. Aunt Belle was right. The circus did leave a baby, but whom did it belong to?

Her mother quickly set her straight. "Here is your new little cousin, Burt," she explained. The little people brought him to Aunt Lois and Uncle Bill because they didn't have any children.

Loraine thought to herself, "That's fine. He looks kind of ugly, but I suppose he will grow up okay. It will be fun to have him next door. I hope he can walk?"

And so it was. The circus came to town every year, but never brought another baby to any of the four houses. This was particularly disappointing to Loraine because Aunt Belle and Uncle Bert needed a child of their own. It would have been nice if the little people could have dropped off just one more baby.

Sitting on the Front Porch

by Loraine Barkham Campbell

An incident in the summer of 1942 has remained vivid in my mind. I can recall exactly how we looked and what our reactions were, but I can only remember parts of the conversations. I'll just have to wing it and use my best recollections. Aunt Lois had a dear childhood friend, Cozette Collins, who was now living in Oakland. The two ladies hadn't been in touch for some time, therefore Aunt Lois was not the least bit suspicious of the soldier who arrived on her front porch, claiming to be Cozette's husband. Cozette had never mentioned him, but maybe the marriage had happened recently. The young corporal looked fairly decent and sincere so Aunt Lois suggested they sit down on the porch and get acquainted. She was very good at interrogating anyone, but I am not sure how much information she gleaned from this conversation.

At one point, the soldier asked to use her bathroom. During that time she called mom and me from next door to meet him. We chatted and then Aunt Lois offered him some lunch. They went inside and mom and I left.

Aunt Lois was a very good cook, and I'm sure she whipped up an excellent meal. The soldier stayed quite a while, but just before leaving he asked to use her bathroom once more. Then he left, never to be seen or heard from again.

The next morning, and I am sure it was a Saturday, Aunt Lois was getting dressed for shopping. After looking in one of her jewelry boxes she discovered two diamond rings were missing. She was very upset and yelled out her kitchen window for us to get over there fast. We had no idea what had happened to her. We ran next door.

My mother always got right to the point. "Lois, what in the hell is wrong? Are you sick or what?"

Lois replied, "No Alice, I'm not sick. That corporal who was here yesterday stole two of my diamond rings from the bedroom, and I'm sure he was NOT Cozette's husband. But how did he know my name and address?"

Alice still thought Lois had just misplaced the rings. We finally realized the soldier must have taken them. Aunt Lois had a memory like an elephant and she knew the location of every piece of her jewelry.

Now for first class detective work: we put our three heads together and decided the best recourse would be to call the Provost Marshall at Chico Air Base. The army had just completed Chico Field a few months before. It was now a basic training school for future military pilots.

When Aunt Lois called they were very helpful and said they would send someone to her house immediately. The three of us went out to wait on her front porch. Aunt Lois sat on the lawn swing by herself and mom and I occupied those bouncy metal chairs that everyone owned during 40's and 50's. They had tubing that wrapped around, but no back legs. If you bounced hard enough, I think you could have launched yourself into space.

We talked for quite a while. Then all at once we heard a loud crash. Mom and I looked at each other exclaimed at the same time," What was that?" We looked toward Aunt Lois to see what she thought and there she was sitting on the swing's cushions. Only now they were right on the concrete porch. Both of the chains supporting the swing had snapped and dropped her down. Luckily, the cushions went with her. There she lay, sprawled with her legs jutting out like two giant sausages. Aunt Lois didn't exactly have shapely legs, and this was not a pretty sight to behold. At least, she didn't seem to be hurt.

Of course, Aunt Lois and I started into of our laughing spells. By then, it was impossible to gather enough strength to move her. So there she sat, looking ridiculous.

Mom kept glancing down Ninth Street and could see a military jeep coming in the distance. She kept reprimanding us. "I see the man coming from the Air Base. Get yourselves in hand. Loraine, stop laughing. Lois get off those cushions. Stand up!"

Sergeant French pulled up at the curb, got out of his jeep and looked at the tableau displayed before him on the porch.

I know what he must have been thinking. "This group is crazy. Those two older ladies think they've been robbed and the younger one can't stop laughing. Oh, well, it's all part of my job and I'll just try to help them."

Without cracking a smile, he came toward us and accepted the explanation that the porch swing had just broke. He helped Aunt Lois up and into a chair. Sergeant French got out his official notebook and jotted down all the details of the great jewel robbery. Then, Aunt Lois showed him the bathroom and adjacent guest bedroom where she kept her jewelry. She gave him Cozette's address and phone number. He said his goodbyes and waved as he left in his jeep.

The sergeant phoned Aunt Lois a couple of times with a progress report, but needless to say the case was never solved. After sixty years, I can't recall if they ever found Cozette. Nor do I know if she was actually married to the soldier. But I do know the corporal made off with her rings, and we all learned a good lesson. "Stand guard, when a stranger uses your bathroom!"

Reading *Grapes of Wrath*

by Loraine Barkham Campbell

Louise assigned this topic: Read a book or name a movie that meant something to you and why.

I believe I read *Grapes of Wrath* sometime during my early college years. My Grandma Barkham lived next door to me and she and I took turns reading to each other. If I had an assignment to work on at the same time, then it was her turn to read. We knew about the Dust Bowl, especially in Oklahoma. We heard how people lost their farms, piled into old jalopies and headed for California to follow some kind of dream. There were promises of many jobs, but once they got here there was nothing. It was an unbelievably sad story and yet they hung onto hope.

Reading *Grapes of Wrath* was one experience, but seeing it all at the movies in the stark black and white was a rude awakening. I can't begin to tell you how many times I have watched it on TV.

My Grandma and Grandpa's house was definitely marked by the hobos who road into town in boxcars. We lived quite a distance from the railroad station and yet somehow they found us. Those men were always given odd jobs to do, had a couple of good meals and they slept on the hay in the horse barn. Sometimes they lingered on for a couple of days, but we never discovered where they left their mark for the next hobo coming into town.

In 1940 during my first year of teaching, I found out we were required to visit the home of each child in our class. That meant around 36 to 40 home calls and afterwards we were required to write a paper on each case. It was an eye-opener when I discovered three of my students were from genuine "Okie" families who had migrated west. I can't remember where Lara lived, but she had a headful of lice. Faye Bailey and Odell Yearry lived at the city dump in tarpaper shacks and huge packing boxes. They attended school while their parents worked in the olives, peaches and apricots.

Those were the days when we did not have school cafeterias or additional food for these poor children. Fay was often sick, threw up and had no energy. I didn't have the slightest idea what she had eaten to make her so ill. I can never forget those children or the book that was written about them and their families. Eventually, they moved on to another town, another crop and hopefully to a better life.

Chuck Chaffin

I grew up everywhere. Some years were spent in the heartland of Missouri, Kansas, and Nebraska. When we finally settled in California in my junior year of high school, my mom told my dad that she wasn't moving anymore. That felt so good I thought I had just received a summons from the Promised Land.

Arkansas was my birthplace, and until the family moved to Albuquerque, I didn't know I had a southern accent. The soldiers of World War II told me.

I started to work in Albuquerque. I was nine years old, and I made $6.00 a week selling the popular magazines of the 40's – Colliers, Liberty, Saturday Evening Post, and Life. We were poor, and my mom needed the money.

The other side of my life was going to school. I got decent grades, found algebra easy, and did well in Spanish and Latin. However, the dominant theme of my growing up was how much I worked – every day after school, full days on the weekends, twelve-hour days in the summer – shining shoes, washing dishes, cutting lawns, and delivering newspapers.

If you were to drop in my home-office, you would see four college degrees hanging on my walls. A casual glance would tell you that I am an educated man. If you looked at the books on my bookshelf, you would find two authored by me, <u>101 Ways to Answer Your Telephone</u>, and <u>Climate in 3-D</u>. These books would tell you that I've been interested in writing for a long time.

What you might really enjoy looking at, however, are my photo albums on display in my living room. You will see pictures of my two girls from the time they were very young. You will also see me in various settings with my seven grandchildren. From reflecting on these pictures, you will see that I like porch swings, pralines ice cream cones, bedtime embraces, every hand-holding time, sofa time, snuggle time, every soft kiss (long or short), and every, "I love you."

Knowing that about me is as important as knowing that I taught fifth grade for 39 years, that I had four siblings, that I belong to two writer's groups, and that I have many doors in my life that open to special rooms. If you read my stories, you will know what I mean.

I met Louise at South Bay's Musical Theater's 50th anniversary. I had taken a seat at one of the dining tables, and Louise wandered by looking for a place to sit. I suggested that she sit next to me. She hemmed-and-hawed and thought it over, finally, deciding to sit next to me. During our conversation, she told me about the Memoirs group and invited me to come. That was probably two to three years ago, and I have been coming ever since. I enjoy coming, sitting next to Deb, listening to the stories and sharing mine.

Traveling With Mom

by Chuck Chaffin

My mom never expected to be much of a traveler. She didn't travel much of anywhere until she was twenty-seven. Then everything suddenly changed. She moved to Joplin, Missouri, with my dad and their three young children, ages one to four. Two years later she was living in Pittsburg, Kansas, and two years after that, it was Rogers, Arkansas, but her real travels began in 1943 when she was thirty-seven. By then, she had five children, ranging in ages from four to thirteen.

We were living in a little, boxy, two-bedroom adobe house in Albuquerque. The house wasn't much. My single bed was shoved up next to an outside wall in the living room. My two brothers and two sisters slept in the front bedroom. One bathroom was shared by all of us. The kitchen, as little as it was, had space for a small kitchen table. I remember sitting at that table one night eating cold oatmeal patties for dinner. As cramped and confined as the house was, it was better than anything we would have for the next year.

My dad was living in Phoenix, and in the spring, Mom visited him. It was then that she made the decision to move the kids and join him there. Selling the house, pulling up stakes, and moving to Phoenix in the middle of summer was not a smart idea, but we did it anyway. That was the first of eight moves that year.

Mom herded all five kids down to the Greyhound Bus Depot where we boarded a bus bound for Phoenix. Mom was young and attractive, and no one could believe that all those kids belonged to her. The trip was fairly easy, for not many people were bound for

Phoenix in August. I don't know what we did for luggage. The only suitcase I ever remember seeing at home was Dad's old, scuffed up, brown leather suitcase. I have a hunch that my mother packed whatever few clothes we had in boxes.

Phoenix turned out to be too hot for Dad, especially since he worked in a bakery, making it even hotter. He had a constant heat rash and soaked in Clorox baths to fight the irritation. It didn't work, so my dad got another job – this time in Kearney, Nebraska. As the saying goes, "If you can't stand the heat, get out of the kitchen."

After living in Phoenix for a month, my mom once again loaded the children onto the Greyhound Bus. We were on our way to Kearney. It was 1943, and the country was at war. Gasoline was rationed, so people had to rely on bus and train travel. The buses were crowded, and I sometimes doubted if we would get on board. Every seat was taken, and small folding seats were placed in the aisle. If you nodded off, you would fall off your little seat. I remember sharing a regular seat with my youngest sister. We were crammed in together, so whoever dozed off first got the lion's share of the seat.

It was a long and tedious journey from Phoenix through Flagstaff and Albuquerque to Santa Fe, Denver, and Cheyenne, and finally to Kearney. One of the children was frequently irritable. Another one, when my mom wasn't looking, kept fooling around, trying to entertain whoever was nearby. Then there was the one who always had to go to the bathroom. I spent my time staring out the bus window, taking in the farmlands, admiring the rolling landscape, and wondering who lived in the houses. It would have helped if we had books or games to entertain us. Not having either, Mom had her hands full.

When we arrived in Kearney, we had no place of our own to go to. A few of us stayed with the family who owned the bakery and their four children. The rest of us were farmed out somewhere. This arrangement didn't work at all, so after one week, Mom told Dad,

"You get us better housing, or we're going back to Phoenix." A second week passed. Nothing happened, so my mom put us back on the Greyhound Bus and headed us back to Phoenix. A map at the bus station showed every Greyhound depot in America, hundreds of them, and the way things were going, I thought we would ride through every one of them.

Back in Phoenix, we lived in a motel on the highway, and I enrolled in 7th grade. Two days later, we got a call from Dad. He had found housing in Kearney, so once again, we were back on the bus. We no longer needed a rudder, a compass, or a joy stick to chart our jagged way northward. By now, the stars knew us, so the North Star became our guiding light, and if the bus driver got lost, I could give him directions, for the route was now as familiar to me as the back of my hand. Some of the busses were old and creaked along, straining to make up the steep mountain passes. The cornfields of Nebraska were endless, and the small towns were far apart, but the bus and the driver stayed with it, as the old vehicle chugged noisily along, finally dropping us off in Kearney.

We children were still occasional nuisances to each other, some taking up too much space in our shared seats, and, generally, not knowing what to do with ourselves. However, we were quite well behaved. We didn't chase each other around the lobby of the bus depot, call each other names, or shove one another. There was no yelling when we didn't like what was happening. Nobody tried to break into the candy machines, or act out any awful kid behaviors. My mom was a no nonsense mom who kept her children in line and wouldn't allow too much horse play. Still, my oldest sister, Mary, was embarrassed by the size of our family. It was during the war, and many soldiers were on the buses. I'm sure that many of them did a double take when they noticed Mary. She was 13, pretty and beginning to develop. All part of a young soldier's dream.

Our first house in Kearney was unfurnished. Not having any furniture, we slept on the floor. It wasn't long before we moved into a private home with furnished rooms upstairs. The new quarters were tight and crowded, but still somewhat adequate. We had Thanksgiving there, but my mom was notoriously late with Thanksgiving meals. Late that afternoon, my dad grew tired of waiting. So he got upset and left. I don't know where he went. Kearney was a small town of 10,000, and Thanksgiving is a family holiday, but he obviously had a place to go. His impatience, anger, and abandonment cast a gloom over the rest of the day, but it was nothing new, for he had done it many times before.

About this time, a home across the street had a furnished upstairs unit that became available, but the landlord had never rented to children. My mother convinced her that her children were well behaved. This place was bigger, and we had space to spread out. There was even a quiet space for me to read on Friday nights. I thought we were finally upscale. Mom's reward had come. Her joy returned, and for awhile, she had won.

I had one of my best Christmases in that house. We had a tree, and my dad was home. It snowed that holiday, and the children and Dad frolicked in the snow, building a snowman, a snow fort, and throwing snowballs at each other. Even though there were more good times that year, living in Kearney had its challenges. Celia, age 11, had to walk my dad's lunch to the bakery before school. This sometimes made her late for school, and one time hurrying on the snowy, frozen sidewalks, she fell and badly sprained her wrist. Bill, six, like John in Phoenix, had the measles. The house was quarantined, and a warning sign was posted on the front door.

It snowed a lot that year. There were many days that Mary and I trudged through deep snow, walking the mile to school. At times, the winter was unbearably cold. It was tough on my mom. She did the family washing across the street and had to hang the clothes on an outside line. Her hands couldn't take the extreme winter cold. With five children and my dad's bakery clothes, washes were done every other day, so Mom was exposed to the snow and cold several times a week. It was the reason we moved at the end of the school year.

We made this trip as a family. We traveled by train, and it was reassuring to have Dad with us. Our next stop was Denver. We lived in the Milner Hotel for a month, and I sold the Denver Post across the street from the main post office. Years later on a return visit to Denver, I searched for the Milner Hotel, only to discover that it was no longer there, having given way to urban renewal.

We left Denver after one month and returned to Albuquerque, the place where it all started. We bought a decent home in a nice neighborhood and stayed put for three years. But that year when I was twelve and moved eight times? What do I make of it? What effect did it have on my emotional stability? Did the year's experiences scar any of my brothers and sisters? Was I part of a crazy, nomadic family? Or was it just the times when women were dependent on their husbands and capitulated to their whims?

The answer to these questions is probably, "Yes." Still, there are probably no definitive answers. Perhaps the main value is to reflect on all the moves and weigh the toll it took on my mom, knowing that she stuck with her husband, my dad, because she saw it as the only way to give her kids the best life possible. I am in awe of her grit and unwavering courage in the midst of overwhelming circumstances. She sacrificed over and over again to keep her family together.

Now it's up to me to learn from that tumultuous year and to engage all my skills to help me carve out the best life possible from my many daily experiences. My mom, along with my growing-up experiences, will be there showing me the way.

Mom had *whatever it takes*. Will we get on this crowded bus? *Whatever it takes*. Where will we live? *Whatever it takes*. I'm tired, Mom. *Whatever it takes*. Inconvenience? Stamina? Pushing on? Fatigue? *Whatever it takes.* She had to do it all alone. She couldn't take herself out of the lineup and insert a sub. There weren't any. She was a team of one – player, coach, manager, referee – playing every position for the whole game, while at the same time doing all the officiating. She could never call a timeout and regroup. Every day she had to refuel and attack, attack, attack. There was never a day off. There was never a time she could kick back and take it easy. Everything, so fragilely held together, depended solely on her. You don't win the ultimate prize if your big horses don't bring it every day, and my mom did. Each and every day she put it over the top and out of the park.

For four long bus trips, she couldn't hiccup or pause in mid-sentence. Everything was decided by a minute-to-minute existence. Not day-to-day, or hour-by-hour, but minute-to-minute. There can be nothing but admiration for someone who puts herself on the line every morning when she's not even close to 100 percent. Her daily challenge was to fix the unfixable. She simply believed that the supernatural was not going to allow her to mess up. If anybody knew how to survive, it was my mom. Every time she stepped on the playing field, she left the angels in heaven gasping, "Did you see that?" *Whatever it takes*.

Remembering Scampy

by Chuck Chaffin

Fourteen blocks east of downtown San Jose, and just two blocks from Santa Clara Avenue, the primary east-west route through town, is the neighborhood of my youth. It is a beautiful tree-lined neighborhood of stately homes and well-manicured lawns. Prominent city merchants and civic leaders lived in these homes. It was one of the prestigious neighborhoods in San Jose.

In this San Jose residential community, memories of my growing-up are everywhere. First, there is the house at 216 South 14th, built in 1906, the year of the San Francisco earthquake It had two sets of steps, one set leading up to the front porch. The ledges on the sides of the steps were used to fold my newspapers.

The featured outdoor activity at our house were the regular one-on-one football games between my two brothers. The front yard, as small as it was, and divided by a concrete sidewalk, making it even smaller, was the site of those games. Before the game began, Bill and John would meet on the sidewalk at mid-field. There would be a serious discussion about rules and playing fair. Then they would flip a coin to decide who would kick and who would receive, shake hands in good faith, go to their respective ends of the football field, and the game was on. Having only one player on each side, my brothers gave new meaning to the term, "a one-man-team."

Even though Hugh McElhenny, Frankie Albert, and Crazy Legs Hirsch never played on our turf, their names were frequently announced over our make-believe loud-speaker system. With my oldest brother calling the plays and impersonating McElhenny, touchdowns were scored often and in spectacular fashion. For one afternoon, Bill lived out the fantasy of every 12-year-old boy who ever cradled a scuffed Wilson football under his arm on America's favorite and most popular gird iron turf - the front yard.

To hear Bill tell it, he was always in the running for national player-of -the-year. However, the games never had any newspaper or radio coverage, so Bill never got any national publicity. In fact, the games barely got any neighborhood notice, even though Bill liked to talk about how the neighbors, hiding behind their curtains, were glued to their front windows, excitedly watching the games unfold.

However, in reality, the only spectator to attend the games was Scampy, John's little black dog. When Scampy curled up on the front porch, he had no idea that football history was being played out right in front of his eyes, as the greatest player on our block worked his never-ending football magic. Whenever a touchdown was scored, Scampy would do this silly yelp, bark his little head off, do spins and run in circles, and, generally, whip the imaginary crowd into a wild frenzy. John and Bill would often suspend play just to watch their one-spectator cheering section. It was all crazy.

The games ended at supper time, and my youngest brother, though gallant in defeat, was left in a daze, not knowing what hit him. As for Bill, he had to check his mojo at the front door and become just another child in our household, doing whatever chores our mom had assigned him

With Scampy, it was a different matter. If he could have gotten into any of those games, he would have left my brothers' heads spinning, because Scampy was fast. Really fast. When he ran, it is reported that his feet barely touched the ground.

I don't ever recall John taking Scampy for a walk. Instead he took him on his afternoon paper route. When John delivered his newspapers, he was a whirlwind, racing up and down the streets on his bicycle, porching his papers in record time. However, no matter how fast John went, Scampy always kept up, sometimes even setting the pace, but most often just content and happy to be by John's side.

However, speed was not the only quality that attracted people to Scampy. Aside from his jet black coat, the first thing you noticed about him was how short he was. He probably measured only 11" tall. He was friendly and obedient, and liked to be petted and scratched under his neck. There was no other dog in the neighborhood more loyal than Scampy, and he was forever devoted to John. If you needed someone to defend you, Scampy would fiercely stand his ground against Great Danes and other big dogs that wandered through our neighborhood.

John, my youngest brother, used to get on his bike and race down our long driveway, yelling either "Hi-Ho Scampy, Away," or "Roll 'Em, Scampy." (Either way, they were good imitations of The Lone Ranger and Red Rider.) Scampy would take up the challenge, racing lickety-split down the driveway, skidding sideways on all fours as he hit the sidewalk. It was great fun for both my brother and his little dog, as both John and Scampy took on the airs of big-name cowboys, rescuing the downtrodden and defending the truth.

Scampy was an outside dog. As such, he spent his nights on his blanket in the detached garage with the rats, mice, and fleas. It bothered John that Scampy had so many fleas, but we were a poor family and couldn't afford more than soap and water. Scampy liked being as physically close to the family as possible. During the day, he slept either at the back door or on the front porch, depending on where the family was. On warm summer days, with the front door open, Scampy would curl up on the porch next to the door, just like he was a member of the family. If John could have changed it, I'm sure he would have made Scampy an inside dog and an honorary member of the family, perhaps even allowing him to sleep in his bedroom at his bedside at night.

The neighbors weren't as fond of Scampy as we were. Scampy annoyed them with his endless barking, especially in the early morning hours when the garbage trucks made their rounds. We think the neighbors eventually silenced the little pup with some food poisoning. John put his sick little dog inside his paper bags and peddled him to a downtown vet. There was nothing the doctor could do. It was a tearful goodbye for my brother. He built a small coffin, painted it white, and buried Scampy in a nearby vacant lot, alongside Coyote Creek near Motorcycle Hill, where on warm, windless summer nights he could listen to the purr and roar of the motorcycles. As John placed a home-made cross on the burial site, he watered the grave with his tears - the tears of a young boy saying goodbye to his best friend.

Me, the Substitute Teacher

by Chuck Chaffin

When does a person move from the mind to the heart? Today's story dances around that question. The answer is important, because when I think (the mind), I don't feel, but when I feel (the heart), I get well. In searching for answers to the questions, perhaps you can give me some pointers at the end of the story.

After I retired, I was a substitute teacher for five years. Being a substitute teacher was like taking castor oil, good for me, but terrible going down. Substitute teaching helped me peel back the layers of who I am. The challenges of subbing helped me focus on what was important – the students and how I interacted with them. If I allowed myself, my mind could wander through the mazes of student thinking all day long, the payoff being unpredictable rewards.

But first, a recess break. Then we will get back to subbing.

Imagine a reader in the morning, a storyteller in the afternoon, a TV viewer at night, and a gym rat three days a week. Suppose this man, you know him as Chuck, finds the major areas of his life filled with physical uncertainty, mystery, a little bit of messiness, and that nearly every day is an occasion to wrestle with deep questions of getting older and life in general.

Author C.S. Lewis used a tactic he called "the supposal" in his writing to ask a series of "what if" questions. When he posed the question, "Suppose that God's reconciling work happened not in our world but in a fanciful world?" The *Chronicles of Narnia* were born.

I always thought it would be easy to become a writer. There are so many stories to write and so many characters to write about. But it turns out that, other than a Christmas letter or a research paper for a graduate class, it was much easier to think of myself as a writer than it was to sit down and write.

While I have always been interested in writing stories, I left the writing to others, never putting pen to paper until I started writing daily summaries of the school day's activities when I was a substitute teacher. I always found it more entertaining to embellish the truth rather than write a blow-by-blow account of what happened in reading and social studies, and I could always leave the resident teacher guessing and in suspense when I titled a daily report, ***Stuck between Reading, Writing, and Ambush.*** That's when I learned to love the adventure of storytelling.

"You have characters, sometimes known as students, frequently defined by their own self-imposed prisons. You have a general idea of how things are going to go. There will be interruptions, recesses, and a long lunch break. In-between, chaos could happen at any time. The students are the ones who drive it and make it happen. I especially loved it when they came alive. You start to love them or put up with them, and you feel compelled to get to the end of the story, in this case, the daily report, or you will just leave these poor kids and their teacher in limbo."

I enjoyed the rhythm of subbing, starting the day standing in the doorway welcoming the students, then answering their questions about whether I was funny or not. My answer was always, "Very." While I wore many hats as a substitute teacher, there was a cohesive unity in all I did. It was a place where someone like me, who likes to both kid and deal with the serious stuff of the classroom, could operate at full throttle without ever being kicked out.

I sometimes shared stories of living on my grandpa's farm in the summer where I learned to gather eggs, hoe the fields, plant the crops, harvest the green beans, and pull water up from the well. The students learned from me that sometimes our smallest actions can lead to our biggest victories. I frequently reminded them that despite their fears, they can overcome any obstacle when they understand that they are limited only by their imagination.

Ultimately, like my days in the classroom, I hope my stories in this writer's class allow the readers to wrestle with the hard questions of like, particularly the ones that carry a strong undertow. I would like people who are struggling with loss, heartache, loneliness, and pain to know that they can find meaning in the midst of agony. They can find the truth of life in the most unexpected way and in the most unexpected places. It is a baton worth passing on.

Which is Better, HAPPY OR SAD?

by Chuck Chaffin

When we take inventory of all the moments in our lives, we don't want to overlook the sad moments. In many ways, they mean more than the happy ones. I have had many sad moments, but at the time they happened, I didn't group them into happy or sad, I just lived them.

For me, those moments, both happy and sad, could have been in Albuquerque or Fort Smith, Arkansas, for my boyhood was lived in so many places. It took place in the days of Roosevelt, Joe DiMaggio, and Ebbetts Field. It happened in the days of streetcars, five cent double-decker ice cream cones, and penny post cards. It's a boyhood filled with selling magazines, shining shoes, delivering newspapers and diagramming sentences and learning Latin conjugations. In my home, you would see my two younger brothers and two sisters, one older and one younger. You would see a mom who would move the laundry back and forth between the kitchen table and the sofa, because she never had the time to fold it and put it away. You would be back in a home that didn't have a father much of the time.

Even when my dad was home, everyone was afraid of his angry outbursts. I remember the time when he took my sister and me to the circus. We were living in Joplin, Missouri and I was four. Dad got upset with my sister because she was afraid to watch a clown get shot from a cannon. Then, there was the Halloween parade. The devil in the parade scared me to death. I don't remember if dad tried to comfort us or not. Perhaps he didn't know how, but he was at least trying to be a good dad by taking us to what he thought would be fun activities. Certainly, a mix of happy and sad.

As dysfunctional as my home was, there was a rhythm to it. Maybe even a structure. There were the stories. The hard times. The vacant Christmases. They all affected the way I turned out. Today, I understand them in a way I never understood them before. Perhaps it's because I reflected on them, processed and learned from them.

I have lived long enough to think about all the things that happened in my life. I don't categorize them into good or bad, because I never knew which they are going to be. Instead, I reflect on them and try to learn from them. I have had to walk through many abyss, but I have learned to persevere, there will eventually be a slopping hillside that leads into a meadow where wildflowers grow in abundance. I can refresh myself by pausing long enough to savor the cool air, listen to the sound of the burbling creek, and join the birds in their singing.

It is easy to embrace our days when life is on track. When we have love, goodness, family, and meaning as parts of life, it is easier to navigate around the sadness that we inevitably stumble across. Anguish and sorrow are unavoidable, but so is beauty and magic. If we stick together with our families and friends, we will be able to make better sense of the chaos when it happens, and we will be able to find more joy in the happy moments as they reach out to hold us.

There will be days when everything stops working, including our best intentions and good ideas. These are shipwreck days when all we have is the hokey-pokey. On these days there is not much left, there can still be a small thread that we can pull that will start life vibrating again.

So when we cope with our stresses and illnesses, we might be tempted to ask, "Which is better, happy or sad?" In many ways the question is mute, for it is like asking, "Which is the most beautiful, one ordinary flower or a bouquet, a walk along a flowering trail or sitting on rocks alongside a meandering stream?"

If pressed for an answer to the question, many of us would say that most of the time we find plenty of significance in life as it unfurls in front of us. We do the best we can. We work hard, we enjoy life and we endure. Some days are better than others. During tough times, we look for solace in nature, music, great literature, the quiet satisfaction of our homes, and solitude with our maker. When life goes as it is expected, day by day, with our jobs, our families, and a few close friends we play with, a better question might be, "How am I handling the petty stuff?"

Family Photographs

by Chuck Chaffin

I have now lived in my mobile home for over two years. For two years, I have walked through the same rooms, ate at the same table, taking in the views on the hillside in the distance, and read from the same sofa. Framed photographs of my family, my parents, and my grandchildren fill the flat surfaces throughout my house. I often look at them, recalling earlier times and younger days. I particularly like the side-by-side single pictures of my dad and me, each looking like we were members of the New Jersey Mafia.

There are two family photos hanging in my living room, both professional photos. In the first one, my mom is beautiful, and my dad handsome. They were 29 then. My dad is dapper in his three-piece suit and white shoes. Imagine that, a baker in a tie and a vest? Mom's hair is styled in the style of the day, and she is gorgeous in her large polka-dot, two-piece dress. She is obviously the pretty one in her family of six sisters. My two sisters are beautifully dressed, and I am decked out in a white sailor's outfit with fold-down anklets and matching white shoes. I was four, and although I remember only scattered events of that time, anyone looking at the picture can easily see that we were a happy family.

The second photo was taken twelve years later in San Jose. The family had grown to five children by then. I was 16 and my youngest brother was eight. We are all dressed in our Sunday best, the two girls in dresses and skirts and blouses, the boys in suits and ties, showing off their Windsor knots. I am in the back row dressed in a doubled-breasted dark blue suit. My brown wavy hair was combed perfectly. My parents were 41 and beginning to show some age. My dad looked strong and manly, and my mom's hair was quickly turning prematurely gray. The family had been through a lot of turmoil by then, and we were no longer a contented, happy family. Instead, we had become very dysfunctional.

It is to my mom's credit that she had the foresight to have these professional photographs taken. They represent a vital part of my history, and, if I didn't have them, many parts would be missing. They are located in a spot where I can see them anytime I sit on my sofa. I sometimes study them, reflect on them, remember my youth, appreciate both the good and bad of my parents, and ponder my childhood and teenage years.

Our family albums help us turn the pages and narrate what lay in our pasts. For me, it was Mom's rhubarb pies, sugary, warm milk toast, Parcheesi and Monopoly games, family arguments, household chores, walking to church and childhood friends who came for Sunday dinners. The pictures will remind us that we were once children and that our parents, like us, were once young and vibrant, too.

We need our family pictures, even though they are flat and two-dimensional and may not be true representations of the real thing itself. We need to touch the flat, laminated surfaces and run our fingers over our parents' faces, thanking them for everything they did for us and forgiving them for what they didn't do. We need to imagine that our fingers would settle on real warm flesh, because they are so alive in these pictures.

So I touch the pictures, remembering the feel of my mom's ribs and arms and the skin and muscle of my dad. Then I remember so much of it: the smell of flour my dad seemed to carry on him (After all, he did work in the bakery.) and the beauty in my mom's face. If only I could remember the exact pitch of her voice and the rise and fall of dad's laugh, I would have them back again, even for a fleeting moment.

I close my eyes and lose myself in these and other sensual memories. For a few moments, I ache for my past, all of it, the way people who have lost an arm or a leg claim they can feel that missing limb. I will sometimes bury my head in my hands for a long time, sobbing and quietly crying, recalling my younger years, and overwhelmed by the changes that we go through in life.   The photographs pull me toward a world filled with emotional land mines, memories that can sometimes be too painful to bear.   During those times, my eyes swim in tears, remembering my roots, where I have come from, and what my life was like back then.

I have come a long way since these pictures were taken. I have changed and grown with every year of my life. My experiences have rewired me. They have allowed me to do and think things that were previously thought of as undoable or unthinkable. My experiences have elicited in me new thoughts and new ideas, and they continue to teach me invaluable lessons, catapulting me to new heights and making me less inclined to repeat the mistakes of my past.

Drinking Organic Tea

by Chuck Chaffin

It was a cold day. The pewter sky held the promise of rain. But inside the coffee shop, it was warm, warm from the coffee machines and the steaming cups of coffee and from all the customers crowded at the small tables. I gravitated toward the only empty seat and began to settle in. Squeezed into the table beside me sat a vaguely familiar woman working on her computer. She brushed the long dirty blonde hair off her face. A half-eaten croissant was on the plate before her, and a spicy scent rose from the cup of tea at her elbow. She looked at me and smiled. Then she said, "You are Mr. Chaffin, aren't you? I was a student teacher in your classroom about 20 years ago."

We chatted about her teaching career and about her personal life. She told me everything about herself. How she loved being married and baking cookies on the weekends. How she left teaching after ten years for a successful career in medical sales. She talked glowingly about her two girls who were now in high school. Kate was the freshest-looking person I'd seen in a long time, as if she had just emerged from a long hot bubble bath. She was the essence of what a big hug ought to be. So optimistic. So chatty. So hard to resist. And now, here she was, at Starbucks, sitting next to me, drinking organic tea. Then she asked about me.

"I'll tell you how I see myself," I said. "I like to be by myself, doing what I want, when I want. Except for my own noise, I like it quiet. There are days I think I'm becoming a hermit. I read books and magazines and the news online. I watch too many harebrained TV shows. Otherwise, how do I explain *Gotham*? I write stories,

105

and do a lot of rewrites, and not having any deadlines, I never miss one. I work out at the gym, but only with the pee-wee weights. It's a very sedentary life. And that's essentially who I am, but it may change by tomorrow. Rapidly advancing age is changing me every minute it seems. Every day can be different, but every day can be the same. There comes a time when a person decides he doesn't have to decide anymore."

Kate sipped on her tea, stared into space for a minute, and then said, "Everything is intertwined. Everything is connected. If we think too much about it, it becomes complicated. It's best to go with the flow and the patterns that emerge."

I didn't tell Kate the other things that define me. The things that I am afraid of. Here are some of them. I am afraid of ending up in a wheel chair and not being able to walk anymore. I am afraid of falling. Some of my friends have and the outcome isn't pretty. I am afraid of losing my physical abilities and becoming handicapped. I don't have as much money as I used to have and am afraid of my investments going south, running out of money and not leaving my two girls an inheritance big enough to make a difference. I am afraid of walking in the dark, stumbling and losing my balance. I am afraid that there will come a time when I won't matter to my family anymore. ("Oh, the old man is in an old folk's home somewhere, but still kicking, I hear.") I am afraid of being jostled in crowds and people bumping into me, perhaps knocking me down. And, on a lighter note, I am afraid that my stomach will someday strain against my sweatshirts, but the fear is not big enough to change my snacking habits.

What I am saying is this: As we get older, much of life is coping with our anxieties. Anxieties about disabilities, about handicaps, about relationships, about health, and even the state of the country. It seems like every day holds some danger these days, and if I don't watch mindless TV shows like *Gotham*, I may not find an acceptable, healthy way out.

In summary, I am a single man who lives alone and takes relatively good care of himself, but I am older now and am experiencing the ravages of old age. Sometimes it is a little unnerving. Still, I get myself up every morning, move through the world somehow, and every Wednesday I drive the two miles to my writing class and face the writers in the group. Now that's something to be really afraid of.

Our Memoirs Class

by Chuck Chaffin

Our memoirs class is becoming more than a group of individual writers who share their stories. We are becoming a community. A community that laughs and feels and lets the tears well up in our eyes and silently roll down our cheeks. We support each other with verbal hugs and acknowledging looks, looks that say, "We get it." Even though there are no loud hurrahs, high fives, or enthusiastic back slaps, there could be, for we are beginning to feel that deeply for each other. Maybe we are not like Jesus's band of disciples, but we are getting there, because we are all beginning to wade through the ups and downs of our lives together.

At our last meeting, Leta shared some very moving memories about her late husband, Charles, and Eleane wrote endearingly about her grandson. Her stories about Dillon tell us that one of the gifts our grandchildren give us is to wedge open our hearts to mystery and more tolerance for a different kind of order.

Leta's and Eleane's stories remind us that when you run your hands through the experiences and memories of someone you love, they stick to you, and no amount of licking your fingers will remove their taste. They get in your hair, in your eyes, and in your clothes. They cling and haunt. Stories like these keep me living in wonder. They jog me awake and move me toward greater openness and acceptance. They are like a ballast that keeps me tethered to the earth. It is because of stories like these that I feel like something huge, like a tide, has washed in. We have found our lucky four-leaf clovers, and we will never be the same again.

Our group has everything you might need – fun, friendship, joy, laughter, stimulating stories, and tons of encouragement to help you become the writer you would like to be. And no matter who you might become, we will never use the professional psychiatric term, "cuckoo," to describe you. If necessary, we will be each other's cook, gardener, nurse, companion, psychologist, and biggest rooting section. We will wait in line to serve you your favorite ice cream and cookies. We will always have an unlimited supply of Band-Aids and Kleenex. You never know when you will need one. You only know you will.

As a group, we have lived a long time. Whereas we once had flat bellies, we now have comfortable tummies. Our bodies are beginning to show signs of aging. Still, we have a positive outlook on life, a cozy warmth, and a rowdy sense of humor. We have lived long enough to know that our true beauty is on the inside – in our goodness, that coming here is like a refreshing walk in the early morning or sitting on a front porch swing in the cool of the evening.

Even with all this in our favor, I'm sure there will be times when we can drive each other nuts, especially if someone throws up her arms in desperation and says, "It's the least I can do," and given the right circumstances, I'm sure we can whine and moan until we want to say, "Good grief, Girl, what's wrong with you?"

Burying the Hatchet

by Chuck Chaffin

"Things are not as they seem. Nor are they otherwise."

Louise has been encouraging us to use quotes in our writing, and here I am starting this week's story with a quote. Makes me wonder, "Just how good is this story going to be?" In my last story, I had four quotes, but to start a story with a quote? Whoa. That's as good as having drunken nudes at the beach, even though your preference might be for funny alcoholics.

But let's get back to the quote. "Things are not as they seem. Nor are they otherwise." I have no idea who said this, my preacher or the local drug guy. No matter who said it, I have experienced it many times.

I had an aunt who died last week. She was 99 and four months. She died carrying a lot of grudges to her grave with her. My grandfather provided a burial plot for his family of nine children, but Annie is not going to be buried there. She doesn't want to be buried next to her sister, Opal, so she is going to be buried in the same cemetery, but in a different spot.

I have written stories about my dysfunctional family, but it goes beyond my mom and dad and my siblings. It goes all the way back to Arkansas, and I wonder what made me different. What saved me from the destruction of grudge bearing?

I guess early on I figured out that I could suffer great emotional hurt, or I could have the combo platter. I could hurt, play, cry, suffer, and complain. I could be bruised, confused, ashamed, exhausted, winded, and frozen. All of the above. Sometimes at the same time. I learned that instead of being revengeful, I could help people. Instead of covering my head with itchy burlap and sobbing for long periods of time, I could be mesmerized with life and learn to savor ice chips.

Reading was part of my salvation. Often there was only me, the book, and the space I was reading in. I sprawled in my space, my hands held the book, and I listened to the whisper of the pages as I turned them on-by-one. My heart began to open in slow motion. Old grudges vanished, grievances began to shrink to manageable sizes. I saw people for what they were, twisted and broken, fallen and trapped. No one is any better than anyone else, and nowhere is no better than anywhere else. Humans want and need exactly the same thing: to feel safe, to belong, to be loved, and to be respected. It is so simple, but being human can be so discouraging.

No matter how discouraging it may sound, acknowledging our finiteness is what gives connectedness with others. As hard as it is, all I have to do is let God enter my life as a track coach for slow people and begin praying, not for things I want, but for being changed in ways I can't come close to imagining. It's a prayer I need to pray every day.

The next two stories are *FICTION*. This is Chuck's imagination at work. We would like to provide a couple of examples of a memoir writer and how he can draw upon life experiences and imagination to write fiction.

****

San Jose as Seen in the Phone Book
(Fiction)
by Chuck Chaffin

What does the city phone book tell us about San Jose? I was put on hold the other day, so while I was waiting, I started looking through the phone book to find out.

I became fascinated with the many names. Some are **Short**, like **So** and **Yee**, and, of course, **Short**, and some are longer, like **Strandberg**. It has 10 letters, but **Schindewolf** has one more, 11. **Goodarziardakni** has 15 and is the longest. **Schanzenbacher** is a long name, too. I think I will use it the next time I'm in Starbuck's and the clerk asks me my name. I can't wait to hear the barista yell, **"Schanzenbacher,"** when my drink is ready.

Some people are named after colors - **Brown, Black, Green, Scarlett, Redd, Allred,** and **White.** The **Whites** got carried away with their names. Not being content with just **White,** they added **Whitehead, Whitefeather, Whitebread,** and **Whitehair.** There is also an **Orange**, but she sees herself more as a fruit than a color, which is kind of **Looney**, if you ask me. I would like to talk to **Brownie** to see if he sees himself as a color or a **Treat.** There are no Yellows, Blushes, or Purples, but **Lavender** comes close.

Our city has a **Husmann** (not Husband, silly), but no Wife. I don't know if that is a good thing or **Nott**. The phone book tells us that we have a **Mann** in **Town**, but I was disappointed to find that there is no Woman. However, the **Guys** in **Town** still need to behave themselves, but just in case they don't, we have a **Priest** and a **Pastor** who will help them absolve their frequent or occasional indiscretions, to which the **Lotts** say, "Good Luck."

Day is in the phone book, but Night isn't. However, **Knight** is. There are more **Days**, 11, than there are **Knights**, 4, to which I say, "**Goody.**" And I wonder if we would ever be so lucky as to see the **Knights** around **Town** dressed in their shiny armor and if a **Knight** would ever go out on a **Day** like this? I would also like to ask **Tan** the same kind of question. "Are you **Tan** from the **Sun**, or are you **Buck Rogers** from the **Moon**?"

Names like **Fiddler, Clapper, Hammer, Barber, Farmer, Carpenter,** and **Fisher** tell us what a person does. **Taylor** obviously works with cloth, **Talley** with numbers, and **Gardner** with the soil. Makes me wonder what the **Stoners** do. Do you think they're still on the **Weed**? The same with the **Drinkwaters** and **Rainwaters.** In a year of drought, they better be careful. I have no question about what the **Treats** do. For sure, they will be busy on Halloween.

San Jose doesn't have seasons. Perhaps some would blame this on global warming. However, we do have **Summer, Fall,** and **Spring**, and for me, that's **Goodenough.** For those of you who like to get around, we have the four points on the compass, **North, South, East,** and **West,** to help you find your way. If you want to take a long trip, you **Boys** can travel to **Montana, Virginia, Georgia,** and **Washington.** If you get **Luckey**, you might meet a **Lovelady** and fall in **Love,** especially if she is a real **Angel.** At rest areas, you could curl up in her **Arms** and **Neck** a **Little,** or **Lotz.** Just don't let your **Church** or **Temple** know about it.

Butt and **Dick** have made San Jose their home. I don't know what they do, but I doubt if they would have successful careers as substitute teachers. Not a **Smart** move. We all know what the **Walkers** and **Waddles** do. If you ever see them **Stroll**ing down the **Street**, you can bet **Chase** won't be far behind. Some of the names I like best - **Woody, Wooley, Notti** and **Tweedi** - have such a warm, cozy sound to them.

We have the **Towns** in our **Town**. We also have the **Townes**. Neither group can agree on the correct spelling. **Sandwisch** has the same problem. **Story** and **Storey** can't agree either. I can understand why **Wolf, Wolfe,** and **Wolff** spell their names differently, because **Wolves** aren't known for their spelling. But **Sharp** and **Sharpe** should be **Smart** enough to figure it out. If they can't, we have **Wise** people in our city, plus a few who are even **Weiser,** who can help. The **Tutors** can also pitch in.

The **Bostons** live here. Ask them to say, **"Buttar."** If they feel displaced, they should visit the **Welcomes**. **Bullock** lives here, too, so does **Lincoln, Truman,** and **Adams,** and that's no **Bull**. We also have royalty, as in **Printz** and **King**. Personally, I would prefer a queen, but what the **Heck**. To my surprise, there's a **Waldo** living here. I thought we were still looking for him.

If you are a little **Short** on **Cash**, you can call the **Banks**. They will lend you **Pennies, Nickels,** or even **German Marks**. Just make sure you don't **Cheatam**. Let the **Crooks** do that. Your life will be **Fuller** for it, and in no time at all, you will be a real **Moneymaker.**

For those who play golf, we have a **Parr,** and for football and baseball players, we have a **Field** with a **Diamond**. Maybe you will find **Baldi** there hitting the **Balls**. For our retired seniors who don't want to do much, **Doolittle** will help you out. Call **Dunn** when you are finished. You are **Wright** if you said we have a **Foote** and a **Hand**. We also have a **Butler** who will **Cook** your **Burgers** for you. Just let him know when you are done **Eaton**. The phone

114

directory also says we have **Bacon**, but it doesn't say if it comes with eggs. Maybe just a side of **Ham**.

Our city has **Minors**, and to the delight of the **Biggs**, even if they grow up, we will always call them **Minors**. You might be surprised to know that we have a number of fruits in our town. We have **Grapes, Lemons, Huckleberries, Olives, Berries, Cherries, Dates, Apples,** and at least one **Plum**. The **Nutts** and **Chestnuts** are happy that they are not fruits.

That's a little of what our phone book tells us about our community. Our city has Scandinavians (**Lundstrom**), Germans (**German**), Japanese (**Watanabe**), Chinese (**Shuey**), English (**English**), Irish (**Irish**) and Spanish (**Latino**) all living happily side-by-side in our phone directory. It makes us all **Winners**, and **Wei** are **Better** off that way.

Now for my final remarks. I would like for you to relax and be at your **Leisure** as you enjoy my comments about our group members. I promise to be a good **Steward** with their names.

Our memoirs class meets in a **Hall** made of **Brix**. Even though the place is clean and tidy, you may still find an occasional spider **Webb**. If you don't like our meeting place, you can go hide behind a **Bush** somewhere. No one will **Su** you for it. Instead, we will welcome you back anytime.

Ducks in the Library
(Fiction)
by Chuck Chaffin

He loved the way she said she was from "The Bay Area," and the way she searched the city for a good burrito. She closed her eyes and said she could smell autumn coming, and she always loved autumn. The rains would soon be coming, and she would have to get out her sweaters and umbrella.

She was English. Exactly half. Except for her hair, she did not look English. Her eyes were blue, and she had such fair skin that she always wore a hat in the sun. Today she was wearing a pale pink straw hat with a short brim. It had a black ribbon around it that ended in a triple loop. The small brim made her face look both sophisticated and girlish. Her friends would say, "Well, la-di-da." It was so cool and made her feel very happy. Without question, Julie was glorious and charming. And she was smart. She knew words like missile and non-toxic. She knew her multiplication tables and how to do long division.

Julie was small for her age, and her eyes blinked rapidly and often. She blushed easily and often giggled in her girlish way. Today, she was wearing blue jeans and a soft blue floral print top that had orange flowers floating on an off-white background. She looked irresistible. Her heart was beating a little too fast, the way it always did when she knew something unusual was about to happen.

She sat at a table, drinking a glass of water. Perspiration glistened on her face, which was pink and a little blotchy. Her hair was not quite red and not quite blonde, but somewhere in between, and it hung in a sweaty tangle around her face. She had too many freckles, the kind that make a face look cluttered. All those freckles, and the tip of her sunburned nose, made her seem even younger. She picked up her tattered backpack, the one she used for only special occasions, and tried to look calm. But her heart was beating a little too fast, the way it always did when she knew something unusual was about to happen.

Then the ducks arrived, as they were scheduled to do. The ducks waddled so awkwardly through the library. As they shuffled along, Julie showed them the magazine section and the computer room. She made it a special point to show the ducks the historical room with particular significance given to our country's Thomas's - Thomas Jefferson, Thomas Edison, Thomas Paine, and the fictional, Tom Sawyer. She purposely left out Tom Brady and Tom Cruise, because the ducks thought Thomas was a stupid name. The most exciting room for Julie was the children's room. It had books about everything, including ducks, and today the children's librarian was going to read aloud, *Make Way for Ducklings*. Julie shivered just thinking about it.

When Julie and the ducks were done touring the library, she took them to the library cafe where the ducks could buy bread and leafy greens. She didn't mention that the snack bar also served smoked duck. Instead, she told them that she always gets a baby vanilla ice cream cone.

Then Julie noticed that it was 4:00 o'clock. Her mom would be there any minute, and she would have to say, "Goodbye," to the ducks. When she got home, she would have to practice her violin and later set the table for dinner. When she went to bed that night, she would visit her imaginary animal sanctuary where there are libraries for elephants and giraffes. She would drift off to sleep, counting her chickens, as she wiggled her waddle with the ducks in the library.

Diana Chan

I joined the Memoir class on the recommendation of my line dance classmate, Jean Su.

The attraction of the class to me was the warmth and support of the participants as each person read their story. We give each other constructive feedback and the class creates a safe environment for us to read out loud the stories, and writings about recent or past experiences we have had in our lives. Some of Chuck Chaffin's stories and poems are humorous, some are inspirational, with wise thoughts, pithy sayings almost like Solomon's proverbs.

Louise's suggestion for "A Random Act of Kindness" inspires us to think what we could do to make someone happy. I feel positive at the end of each class having heard someone's personal story, having read mine and received some suggestions, and hope I too will write something significant. I have not contemplated writing a memoir. I am a novice member of the class since February 2016.

I was born in Shanghai, China, lived in Hong Kong, and Brazil, came to the United States for prep school and college earning a BS in Education and my Masters degree in Education, Guidance and Counseling. I counseled high school dropouts in the South End of Boston, became Education Director of Head Start at the South End

Neighborhood Action Program before retiring to become a full time mother. I have a son and a daughter, two grand kids, and we fly several times a year to see our children in Manhattan, New York City. After our children were grown, I worked as a vocational counselor helping Vietnam homeless war veterans.

At 77 years old, my husband and I are retired and empty nested. We've travelled extensively abroad. This year we went to Costa Rica to attend a 75th wedding anniversary of my husband's brother. I just returned from Dubai, Jordan, and Iran. I had several book events at the Los Altos Library, the Los Altos History Museum, at Hakone Gardens, and the Saratoga Library (July) , and at the Asia Society Museum (September) on Park Ave in Manhattan, New York City, to show my recent publication of a children's picture book: ***Animal Kingdom: Vertebrates, Animals with Backbones***. **www.edadventures.com**

I am also the author & publisher of ***Easy 'n Healthy Cooking***, a cookbook with favorite Chinese, Fusion, & Western recipes. **www.easyandhealthycooking.com**

I enjoy line dancing, aerobics, ball room dancing, and playing the piano. It's fun to create healthy recipes and try different types of cuisine after sampling interesting foods at restaurants. I use my books and cooking skills to support community causes as a way of contributing and giving back to the community. It's so true that the pleasure of giving and making a difference in the world is quite rewarding.

Our greatest joy is getting together with our children and grandchildren who grow up so quickly that we try to seize every moment to enjoy them. I want to stay active and continue to travel as long as I am still mobile, and interested.

Animals with Backbones

by Diana Chan

As a newcomer, I am delighted to be in a class with seniors sharing many mutual interests. I am the author and publisher of **Easy 'n Healthy Cooking**, a new genre of Chinese cuisine that incorporates traditional methods of steaming, braising, stir-frying, but no deep frying. My recipes use lean meats, abundant vegetables, and emphasize nutritional value, taste, and good presentation. Most desserts are barely sweet and low in calories, such as the "guilt-free" Cottage Cheesecake & the Bavarian Mousse, an epicurean delight. My website **www.easyandhealthycooking.com** has sample recipes and photos.

My most recent publication, **Animals with Backbones** is a picture book with many fun facts and important educational values for children. It has beautiful photos of Mammals, Birds, Fish, Amphibians, and Reptiles. Under mammals, we have land mammals, including pouched marsupials, and egg laying mammals, then marine mammals. We have a section on Dinosaurs, extinct animals with backbones, clearly shown in the fossils of these giants. Children will understand distinctive characteristics and habitats of animals in each class, and they will learn about endangered animals. Photos were taken in rain forests, national parks, zoos, museums, and in the backyard. There are some extraordinary photos of the

humpback whale, sea otter, and great white egrets taken by semiprofessional photographers.

This book was written with my grandchildren in mind and I have certainly benefitted from the research while doing this project. It has awakened me to the critical needs of endangered animals that desperately need protection from extinction and the unknown future of these wonderful animals.

The rhinoceros, tigers, snow leopards, elephants, gorillas, birds, sea turtles, fish and frogs are fast diminishing in numbers from their loss of habitat, from man's overhunting, overfishing, and the pollution of waters. Climate change resulting from pollution is melting glaciers and creating catastrophic tsunamis, droughts, floods, and hurricanes destroying people's homes, entire villages, cities, and threatening marine animals and wildlife on land.

The leatherback sea turtles, the largest in the world, instinctively go back to the same beaches where they were hatched to lay their eggs. Only one in a thousand survives to maturity as many hatchlings are eaten by birds, fish, land and marine mammals. Unfortunately, man turns out to be their biggest predator as beach fronts are developed into condominiums, which destroy their nesting grounds. Unless many more natural reserves are set aside worldwide, these magnificent turtles are on their way to extinction.

The World Wildlife Fund cites these alarming statistics: "In the past 40 years, over one half of all wildlife populations on earth have disappeared. Simply vanished..." Unless we as parents, grandparents, and teachers work with our children to pass and enforce laws to protect our natural resources, the rivers, oceans, and halt the drilling for tar sand oil creating inevitable risks of spills and pollution, and turn the tide on global warming, and control the pollution of air and water, many endangered animals will go into extinction. We can support WWF (World Wildlife Fund) NRDC (Natural Resources Defense Council) and environment groups, the sentinels that carry enough muscle to safeguard our natural resources and wildlife for our grandchildren's children and the generations ahead.

I am donating a percentage of proceeds from book sales to environmental groups and defenders of wildlife.

My website: **www.edadventures.com** has photos and sample pages.

Easy 'n Healthy Cooking

by Diana Chan

Soon after my son, Derek, got married, he and Rebecca asked me for some fast and easy Chinese recipes. I was thrilled that they actually tried making the dishes and wanted even more recipes which became the genesis of my cookbook, *Easy 'n Healthy Cooking*, a new genre of Chinese cooking using very little oil and no deep frying. Since Rebecca is Jewish, I included Beef Brisket, a Jewish recipe which soon became one of their favorites with minimal effort once the brisket is wrapped and baked, and can be frozen and taken to the ski slopes for a hearty dinner after skiing.

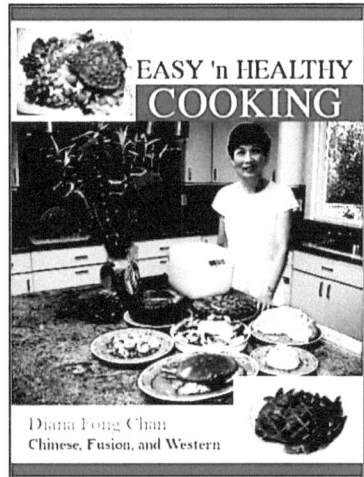

As a child growing up in China and Hong Kong, I never went to the kitchen as kids would get in the way of busy adults. When our family moved to Brazil, I started watching our Chinese cook, a very talented chef who could make dim sum, and elaborate banquet dishes. He skillfully used two cleavers, like a rock drummer beating rhythmic patterns, chopping and mincing meats into pâté in five minutes. He could toss and flip entire contents in a huge wok with his left hand, as easily as the pizza makers toss and flip pizza dough in the air. It was fun watching him as he showed off his cooking skills. Watching him cut, marinate, steam, braise, and stir fry was a natural way learning the basic principles of Chinese cooking, which later facilitated my transition into Fusion and Western cuisine.

You'll enjoy the charming story that goes with Beggar's Chicken. A hungry beggar stole a live chicken from a farmer. In order to hide the chicken and protect himself from being caught, he buried the live chicken in mud. Lacking any cooking utensils, he improvised a clever solution by roasting the chicken encrusted in mud, over an open fire, and enjoyed a deliciously fragrant meal. I pleaded with our chef to make Beggar's chicken, but he never made it for us. The restaurants serve this chicken covered with a terracotta shaped rooster, and they call it "Rich and Famous Chicken" rather than "Beggar's Chicken" so people are more likely to order this special dish.

My mom was always interested in healthy eating, which planted the seeds for me as I am well aware of the benefits of using primary food sources including abundant fresh vegetables, with lean meats, fish and sea foods. I include extra healthy ingredients like apple cider vinegar in salad dressings, and ground flax seeds and wheat germ in some of my latest innovations. My Banana Health Muffins are great for the skin and hair, and beneficial to the digestive and circulatory systems, and a favorite among children and adults alike. I use the color code: red, orange, green, yellow, dark blue, a sure guide to spotting veggies and fruits that are packed with vitamins, minerals and antioxidants.

I love desserts and pride myself in making beautiful and delicious cakes, mousse and ice cream cakes that are barely sweet. I favor baked nuts and snacks that are healthy and crunchy. I like Western desserts that can be made before the party and some can be frozen so that it makes it easy for the hostess to just serve dessert.

The basic principles behind **Easy 'n Healthy Cooking** are very much in line with current nutritional advisories. We know that the foods that are good for the heart are also good for the brain. We are what we eat, so it's wise to make good healthy choices that please our palates and also keep us healthy

N.B. **Easy and Healthy** in Bold letters identify the beginning recipes readers could try as those are really fast, easy, and will get you on a fast track to using the cookbook successfully.

Website: www.easyandhealthycooking.com has photos, reviews, sample recipes.

Highlights of Jordan: Jerash, Petra, Wadi Rum and the Dead Sea

by Diana Chan

We flew from Abu Dhabi, United Arab Emirates, to Amman, Jordan. Driving north to Jerash, to see the Greco-Roman ruins, we were amazed at Jerash's proximity to Syria, just 20 miles to its border. Jerash was one of the major Roman provinces after the conquest of General Pompey in 64 B.C. It is the second greatest attraction after Petra, in Jordan. It is known as the city of 1000 columns. The oval Forum, Temple to Artemis and amphitheater are some of the best preserved ruins showing the elegance of Roman architecture. Hadrian's Arch celebrated the Roman Emperor's visit in 129 A.D.

An earthquake in 749 A.D. destroyed the city and buried it in ashes for centuries until it was rediscovered in 1806, giving it the name "Pompeii of the East." Luckily modern Jerash is built on the outskirts, with minimal impact on the ancient ruins.

Petra, the hidden stone city was awesome. The Nabataeans were extraordinary stone carvers who chiseled the Treasury, a royal burial site or temple out of the sandstone mountain in the 2nd century BC. They were also expert

hydraulic engineers who figured out how to get water into a desert city by harnessing periodic floods and sudden down pours. They built aqueducts, dams, and pipes buried underground along the narrow siq, and channeled the precious and unpredictable water supply to a desert city.

We hiked, rode camels and horses passing cliff dwellings where people lived and were buried. A good guide made our hike more interesting as we admired dramatic soaring cliffs on the way to the Treasury. The Treasury is a monumental façade with columns, an undecorated chamber, and a second story with capital and crest, carved into the mountain. The movie *Indiana Jones* depicted Petra, with a Hollywood version of the Treasury.

In order to reach the Monastery, an even greater challenge above the Treasury, we decided to ride mules up the 800 plus steps thinking that it would save us some strenuous climbing. Little did we anticipate a rollicking rodeo ride as the mules leaped up the steps along narrow cliff paths. Wow, that was some adventurous donkey ride! We were wise to heed our guide's advice not to take the donkey ride on the way down because it would have been too dangerous.

After resting comfortably overnight at the Movenpick Hotel to soothe sore muscles, we drove through Wadi Rum, and soaked in gorgeous desert images, well etched into our memories and recalled similar scenery from *Lawrence of Arabia*. We were descending to the Dead Sea, the lowest elevation on earth, 1407 feet below sea level where the water is so salty (34.2 percent salinity,) that no fish or plants could live. There were beaches with colorful waved sand deposits along the highway as we approached the Dead Sea.

Mud from the Dead Sea is rich with minerals that are good for the skin; so we rubbed mud on our skin, let it dry and then soaked in the Dead Sea where we automatically floated, buoyed by the high salinity of the water. It was a natural spa treatment that helped rejuvenate the skin and soothed the body. It was the biblical health spa for King David and King Harod. We could have spent more time at the Kempinski Hotel which has a private, uncrowded beach, a beautiful swimming pool and view. We spent our time mudding and soaking in the Sea. That was a nice way to relax before we left Jordan for Iran.

Highlights of Iran: Tehran, Yazd, Shiraz, Persepolis, Qom and Isfahan

by Diana Chan

Once we arrived in Tehran, we women had to put on veils covering our heads whenever we were in public places. Golestan Palace, an opulent palace of the royal Qajar family is now a museum showing chandeliers, throne, mirrors, stained glass, carpets, and lifestyle of the ruling kings. It's too bad that the state jewels were kept in the vaults of the Central Bank of Iran with limited display room and no photography was allowed to show the enormous collection of gems and jewelry to rival the British Crowned Jewels and Russia's too.

In Yazd, we had a glimpse of the mountain of silence where Zoroastrians, had strict rules for burial, and beliefs in the purity of fire; believers left the deceased body to be cleansed by the wind and the remains eaten by the birds. Yazd is known for its badgirs, wind catchers, tall towers designed to catch the wind and circulate the air across a pool of water underground to cool the residence of the well to do. It is an ingenious natural air conditioning structure using wind power and water to cool the residence of the wealthy home owners. The Friday Mosque has the tallest minaret towers in Iran with beautiful blue mosaic tiles.

Shiraz is a city that is perfumed with fragrances of flowers or fruit trees that seem to permeate everywhere. Beautiful Eram Gardens, is one of UNESCO World Heritage sites designed with lovely gardens, rock pond and garden. We enjoyed fine dining at Divan, a five star restaurant with ambiance, modern décor, and exquisite Persian cuisine, drinks, delectable entrées and night views of the city. There were adventurous eating experiences at a local tea house where Iranians smoked water pipes and served unique lamb stews. We visited the memorial to Hafez, the famous 14th century Iranian poet and encountered Iranians who gave us freshly picked wild flowers.

Everywhere we went, people of all ages greeted us with smiles, we talked, shared foods, took photos; many students mobbed us for signatures as if we were rock stars. Iranians are as friendly and warm as can be, not the least bit hostile to Americans. They wanted to befriend us and speak English.

Persepolis, the ancient capital of the Archaemedian dynasty of Iran was built by Darius I for ceremonial events in 518 B.C. Darius' son, Xerxes I and his grandson, Artexerxes I, completed the

construction of the capital and the palaces built with limestone, during Persia's most powerful rule. Carvings in stone with subjects and dignitaries bringing gifts, paying tribute to the powerful king reflect the proud display of power of the kings who received the tribute bearers in the Great Apadna Hall with steps so wide that Darius and the Persian royalty could mount the steps on horseback without walking to reach the throne. One of the remaining columns stood a staggering 64 feet high. Many columns were decorated with capitals, tops, carved with two bulls, or eagle heads with the body of a horse, symbols of power in Persian culture. The royal tombs of the kings Darius I, his son Xerxes I, and grandson Artexerxes were carved with façades of a palace with columns into the mountain.

Alas, Alexander the Great sacked and burned Persepolis in 330 BCE and destroyed the grandeur and opulence of palaces and monuments built by those powerful kings. Alexander's army pillaged the treasures and hauled away priceless valuables. How could a brilliant young military strategist and conqueror in good conscience burn and lead the destruction of an empire rich with culture! He and his men were drunk in revelry and committed a cultural desecration leaving only the ruins of the Archaemedian Empire. He is Alexander from Macedonia, not the Great. Ironically, he died seven years later at the age of 32 in 323BC...... Persepolis was destroyed, and the empire he conquered for Greece fell apart. Persepolis was rediscovered in 1601.

Isfahan's Imam Square with the Grand Shah Mosque and the women's mosque, architectural masterpieces, and refreshing fountains in the enormous pool, were built in 1629 ordered by Shah Abbas. It is the symbolic center of the Safavid Empire. The Women's mosque was exceptionally beautiful with indirect sunlight that shined on the peahen's tail in the center of dome. The mosques were decorated with ornate decorated mosaic tiles. We listened to the heavenly call to prayer sung by one of the Iranian tourists who kindly demonstrated the perfect acoustics while he chanted standing beneath the center of the dome. Chehel Sotoun known as 40 Columns Palace with fountain and garden was a pavilion where Shah Abbas II entertained and received guests.

Qom, one of the most religious and conservative cities required us to wear abayas, the cloaks that covered us women from head to toe, just to enter the square. Non-Muslims cannot go into the mosque......so we got a tour from one of the volunteer guides of the grounds and looked at the beautiful minarets and stalactite gold domes, visible from the square. Muslims pray five times a day.

We visited Vank Cathedral, a Christian church built by early Armenian immigrants in Isfahan. There was a memorial to the 1.5 million forgotten Armenians who were killed by the Turks in 1915. We talked with one of the visitors whose grandfather survived the genocide and escaped to Australia.

The caravan serai was a rest stop; inns were built 30 kilometers apart since that was the average distance travelled by camels," the moving vans" that carried merchants and their goods on their hardy backs…The caravan serai were silk route "motels." In contrast we visited the Abbasi House, a wealthy merchant's residence built with the same architectural style as the caravan serai using similar arches only glorified with the addition of wind catchers and landscaped courtyard garden. It was an interesting comparison to dine at a beautiful hotel restaurant with the same architectural style as the caravan serai, only refined with luxurious chandeliers, decorated arches, and stained glass windows and doors.

Isfahan's bridges with arches were lovely gathering places for locals and tourists during the day, at sunset, and at night, lit with scintillating lights. The beautiful Fin Gardens are well remembered for their refreshing fountains, and flowers just as we think of the lovely Persian hotels Abbasi, Espina, Homa's lovely garden.

Aside from the grand mosques, Imam Square, palaces, ruins, beautiful gardens, and adventurous dining, the best memories are the Iranian people's warm welcome. We return as good ambassadors for the Iranian people who love Americans, Chinese Americans. We can tell family and friends that it's safe to travel to Iran. We had fun.

Debby Jacobson Freeman

"On Wisconsin" could be my theme song, as many of my memoir stories take place in my home state from which I moved in 1986.

Since childhood, I have enjoyed writing and reading, but family and teaching career crowded my life. After my retirement in September of 2007, I came to the Memoir class at the Saratoga Senior Center. I had never met Louise Webb, but she was a household name, well known because of her newspaper column in the *Saratoga News.* In her friendly bi-monthly class, Louise has arranged authors to speak, asked motivating questions, and gave valuable writing pointers. Who can forget Louise asking, "Where is the dialogue in your story?"

Each class begins with Louise promoting a book to read. She believes the more you read the better you write. Twice a year the class holds a party that promotes togetherness. In our class, you learn about different locations around the world: New York City, Missouri, Taiwan, Cambridge,

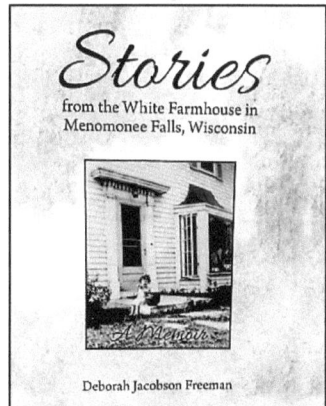

Stories

from the White Farmhouse in
Menomonee Falls, Wisconsin

Deborah Jacobson Freeman

Massachusetts, Cleveland, Ohio and Chico, California as classmates relate their memoirs.

My goal has been to compile a childhood memoir for my three children and four grandchildren about me growing up on a Midwestern farm. *Stories from the White Farmhouse* is available on LuLu.com.

General Science

by Debby Jacobson Freeman

In 1959, all freshmen were required to pass a general science course at MFHS. Science was an educational motto as Russians had surprised the United States in the space race.

My science class was held in a square first floor room, with a row of glass blocks that filtered the light. These glass blocks would prevent me from gazing out the windows. In the front of the room was a dusty blackboard aching to be replaced. Other freshmen sat behind two person glossy black covered tables. They acted like caterpillars wiggling about, ready to morph into butterflies. I was curious as in grade school, the science book gathered dust in my desk.

Crew cut Mr. Wentz, who seemed only a few years older than his students, placed his brief case upon a larger front table where science experiments might be staged. At the left of his table was a tarnished sink and curved faucet. Could chemicals mix on this platform?

During the first months there were no experiments. Mr. Wentz with a kind smile taught from a tired textbook. For his students, general science was the home of vocabulary splattered across the blackboard.

All we did was answer questions at the end of each chapter. Memorization of the boldfaced words in the text was required. I needed more pictures in the textbook.

For our first test, Mr. Wentz created fill in the blank questions. It was like stabbing at words in the dark. How did all those words connect together: water velocity, fluids, heat transfer and mass flow? Multiple choices would have given me a chance.

At home, I studied science at my desk listening to the radio. I knew all the lyrics to *"The Battle of New Orleans"* by Gary U.S. Bonds. "In 1814 we took a little trip," What a great way to remember history. If only there was a top ten song with science terms!

The best part of the class was Terri Johnson, the vivacious freshmen class president who was my table partner. Her blond bob swirled as she talked to me. She was a popular cheerleader who was dating a basketball player. Her face was like a magnet. We were probably placed together as Jacobson and Johnson were in alphabetical order, but I felt esteemed to be her tablemate.

I had never met Terri before this year, as she attended St Anthony's not my Lincoln Grade School. In eighth grade, I could point out the science nerds, but in high school I was flooded with new classmates of various academic ability.

What I remember most about Terri Johnson is that I copied from her test. Yes, I admit this transgression. I knew copying was wrong. My mother was a teacher who shared stories of mischievous students trying to cheat.

During our first test on water and heat, I bumbled through the first nine questions, but on number ten, I drew a blank. I had no idea which science word fit the puzzle. I did not immediately copy Terri. I drilled into my brain trying to find a science term. Fearing to leave a blank on my test, I glanced over at her purple mimeographed paper. Her neat handwriting was easy to read, so I copied her answer. When I finished, I looked at the answers. Did this sound correct? Just then Terri turned and smiled at me. Oh, that girl must be correct, she is so pretty.

About two weeks later, Mr. Wentz asked Terri and I to stay after class. I took a deep breath and followed Terri to his desk. In his hands, he held our tests, with number ten circled in red. The sweat in my armpits began to challenge my deodorant. I forced a serious face pretending I did not know what was to happen. Terri would realize that I had copied, what would she think of me?

Alone in his room, he asked what we were thinking when we wrote our answers. He did not raise his voice, his smile disappeared, and his brown eyes drilled into my body. I had only copied one word. The rest of the test came from my mushed musical brain.

"The two of you have the same wrong answer about the efficiency of heat transfer," he declared pointing to our tests.

Terri spoke first. "I thought refrigeration was a good answer, but I guess that it isn't a scientific term." Her face seemed intent and her blue eyes glistened.

I nodded too. Believing silence was the best alternative. Maybe he did not know who copied whom.

After a pause that seemed forever, he declared. "Girls, you had better study harder as your answers are silly."

Terri and I hurried out of the room together and never mentioned this event. I assumed she realized that I had copied her, but she did not point her finger at me. Maybe she was embarrassed because of her silly answer. Our friendship survived this water and heat transfer problem.

In the end, my science grade was a C, and Mr. Wentz did not call my mother. Terri eliminated a black mark on my file for which I will always be grateful and I learned it is better to be dumb than to cheat.

What Are the Chances?

by Debby Jacobson Freeman

When the wedding invitation arrived, we were perplexed at the location. Not knowing the state of Washington, we checked an atlas to find Semiahmoo Resort in Blaine, Washington. It was a 1/8 inch away from the Canadian border in the Atlas on a peninsula.

Of course, we had to attend, as we had been present at Jacob's sister's weddings. It looked like the cheapest flights were to fly Alaska Airlines into Seattle. Then as a treat we flew to Victoria, British Columbia before attending the wedding.

Well, the wedding was beautiful on the patio facing the water. Even though huge fires raged in Washington, we never smelled smoke. We left the peaceful peninsula on Sunday early so we would arrive ahead of our scheduled flight to San Jose.

After turning in our rented car, we took the Budget shuttle to the airport. Now, we smelled smoke and saw hazy clouds. Inside the busy Seattle airport we walked to Gate 15 where our flight would leave in an hour and a half.

At Gate 15 a plane had just arrived and passengers were entering the waiting area. I glanced up at the line of people and noticed a small curly haired boy that resembled my grandson. THEN I looked at the passengers walking with him.

WONDERS OF WONDERS, that little boy WAS my grandson followed by his sister, Gaby, my daughter, Dulcy and her husband Kelly.

"Hi Nana and Bapa," announced my grandson. My daughter, who was checking her Cell phone as she walked, thought he saw an older couple that resembled his grandparents. Then she looked up and saw her own parents.

GOOSEBUMPS! Of course, we talked and hugged. They were on their way to Spokane to visit Kelly's uncle.

We had not talked with them for a week, as our Cell phone usage in Canada was expensive. Neither of us knew we would be here.

They had an hour and a half between planes on Alaska airlines too. We ate lunch together and could not stop smiling and shaking our heads. Then after giving the children Tee shirts and pencils from Canada, we hugged goodbye. This could never happen again!

Music Story

by Debby Jacobson Freeman

In my baby book that my mother religiously kept, is a notation about her eighteen-month old daughter. "She hums. She claps her hands and wiggles to the music," wrote my mother.

I was surrounded with music as I grew up. The first song I sang by myself was *"Cruising Down the River on a Sunday Afternoon."* It did not matter that we did not live on a river or even own a boat; I just liked the rhyming words and simple tune.

At naptime, my father serenaded me with *"The Bear Goes Over the Mountain to See What He Can See."* I copied him and learned to sing off-tune.

"The Jacobson's cannot carry a tune," Mom would laugh.

My mother had 78 rpm records of Frank Sinatra singing, *"Begin the Beguine,"* which I think she played weekly for a year. To this day, I can identify the first four notes of that song. I guess I would be good at the "Name That Tune" game show.

Off tune singing never stopped me, as I was skillful at remembering the words. My mother owned the musical score of *OKLAHOMA* and played that record daily one summer. My favorite tune was *"I'm Just a Girl Who Can't Say No."* I pretended I was Annie singing the song to the audience.

In my teen years, memorizing all the words of rock songs was more important than learning geometry theorems. Frankie Avalon, the Beatles, and the Beach Boys captured my heart. To this day I can identify the first chords of the tunes like, *"Venus," "I Want to Hold Your Hand"* and *"California Girls."*

To sum up this story, I sing, "Put another nickel in, in the nickelodeon, all I want is loving you and music, music, music."

Joan Gomersall

My experiences with my seven children, 18 grandchildren and one great grandson, create inspiration for my writing. I bring them into my storytelling as well as my historical tales from my childhood and adult life. It seems stories are dedicated to bringing those memories into the future for my family which prompted me to attend memoirs class for 17 years.

Writing letters weekly to my mother over 2500 miles away, when I was raising my children, gave me an incredible foundation to begin sharing my experiences. My 20 years as a second and third grade teacher in two different schools also speaks to my commitment in teaching the next generation of our communities.

Having earned my Bachelor's Degree in Education at Western Reserve University, I went on to obtain a Master's Degree in Education in California. I have served leadership and volunteer positions in many prominent organizations including Saratoga Sister City, Student Exchange Program, Historical Preservation Commission, and Saratoga Taiko, in addition to raising my children and full time teaching positions. I was also, sole proprietor of my antique shop for several years.

A love of traveling since childhood has led me to explore over 90 countries over the past 35 years, as well as ten trips across the United States prior to age 40, with all seven children. I always kept a journal detailing my travel experiences. With my encouragement, my grandchildren also journal their travels and write their own stories. By storytelling I have instilled the "travel bug" into many of my children and grandchildren, as well as several of my students. I have always been the "Giver of books" in the family and community, showing all readers how to use the mind to explore.

Snow Caves

by Joan Gomersall

When I hear about all the snow and freezing weather in the country, it reminds me of when I was growing up. It was in the winter and I was in junior high. We lived on the shores of Lake Erie, outside of Cleveland, Ohio in Willoughby.

Several years we had cold enough weather to freeze the Lake. Along the shore the waves seemed to freeze in mid-way or mid-air, which produced snow caves. My brother and I loved to walk along what was the shore and explore the caves. The other friends in our neighborhood would go with us and we would hide in the caves or walk on

Snow Caves on Lake Erie
Courtesy of photographer, Iusetano:
Hans Huisbrink

top of them. Some of the caves would crumble if the snow was thin. This was our winter sport other than belly slamming down our hilly street. I remember from this sport, I split my chin open and had to get stitches.

Another sport, besides hiding in caves, was to walk out on the ice. Some of the kids went a ways out until they heard the intermittent sound of the ice cracking, which made them turn back

144

to safety! We all knew the dangers of thin ice. The further out we walked the ice would be thinner and the water underneath deeper. But my younger brother had to be different.

One day, he kept walking and played his own game of chicken. We were all screaming at him to come back. The ice was cracking repeatedly but he pretended not to hear us and kept walking. Inside of me I didn't know what to do. Yelling at him was not the answer, so I turned around to leave and not pay attention to him and so did the other kids. Without attention he decided to turn around and come back to shore where it was safe. I was the perpetual "scaredy-cat" and would never do anything dangerous. I was on the shore the whole time worrying and screaming at the other kids.

Things Changed a Lot in 1942

by Joan Gomersall

We used to play on the rug in front of our console radio so we could listen to it while we played. One Sunday night my Aunt, Uncle and cousin, who was three years older than me, were visiting. Our parents were playing cards and my brother my cousin and I were sitting in front of the radio playing with small toys. It was the habit of my parents to listen on Sunday nights to Gabriel Heater, a news reporter. When he came on we were told to be quiet. And one night we all heard the announcement of the Japanese bombing Pearl Harbor. Since we were in Cleveland, Ohio the time difference between Hawaii and Cleveland was about six hours so if it was seven at night it was one in the afternoon in Hawaii. It was a current news story.

Obviously, our life changed after that, our country was at war. Raising money for the war was a big promotional effort. An advertisement on a big Uncle Sam sign encouraged everyone to buy war bonds. At the schools there was a campaign to buy war stamps at a lesser price and when you filled a book you could trade it in for a bond.

There was also an Uncle Sam sign encouraging people to enlist in the service and there was some competition between the different areas of service. Like the Army, Navy and the Marine Corp. Other signs I remember were, "Fight the Axis," with pictures of the leaders of our enemies, Mussolini, Hitler and Hirohito.

Satin signs would hang from the windows of homes where families of soldiers or servicemen lived. The signs would have stars (sometimes several) representing soldiers serving in the war. The stars were in color unless a soldier had died, then it was changed to gold. My brother and I would walk down the street everyday as we went to school and count the houses with stars on the satin signs. Once in a while we noticed a colored star had been changed to gold.

I was eight when I got Scarlet Fever and I was in third grade so it must have been 1943 or the spring of 1944 when my mother came to my bedroom and told me my father had gotten a draft notice. He had already left the bank where he worked and started working in a factory. He was a married man with two children and he was 36 years old. There was a lot of anxiety in our family and I remember my dad and mother going to the bank putting everything in my mother's name and making other financial preparations. Then the day came when my father had to report for duty. He came home and said he was going to be in the Navy because he had flat feet and couldn't march. He was given the date of his departure and everything was ready. President Roosevelt came on the radio and said that men over 35 years of age, with more than two children, would not be drafted. What a reprieve. A day I still remember and I remember the relief of my mother.

The songs on the radio were usually the songs to raise our spirits for the war or love songs. The movies were musicals with lots of pep and color. Many of the movie stars were on trips to war zones or camps to cheer up the soldiers. Bob Hope was one of the most celebrated entertainers who continued going to the soldiers for many years.

I had an uncle in the air force and I thought he was so handsome in his uniform. I thought all the young men were because boot camp put them in good shape and posture.

I remember my brother and I playing in the back seat of my grandfather's Model T Ford. Sometimes we played in the front seat and pretended to drive, but today we were playing that we were being chauffeured someplace wonderful. The model T was in our

147

garage behind the house where we lived. It was basically being stored there because my grandfather didn't drive much anymore. That was because he needed gas stamps for gasoline and all the cars had stickers A, B, or C, in the window for the kind of priority they had for gas. On occasion, my father would start it up and maybe only go out the driveway and back again. To start the engine there was a crank that he put in the front somewhere and turned it until he heard the engine start.

A lot of things were different during those days. I remember belonging to the Campfire Girls and going to roast hot dogs at a day camp one summer. Each of us had to bring our own one or two hot dogs. This was again because we needed stamps for meat. My mother gave me two tokens and some money to stop at the meat market on the way to the meeting place.

We had stamps for shoes, sugar, meat, and for gas. Those are the things I remember. Making margarine was a weekly chore. We didn't have butter very often. My mother would buy a package of margarine and we had to mix in the yellow color with the mixer.

We got most of our vegetables from our Victory garden. Workplaces would find some acres out of the city and let the employees have plots to grow vegetables. I remember going to the garden and meeting other people and playing with other children while our parents did the work. There was a social aspect to it and a competition for biggest vegetables and neatest garden as well as supplying others and ourselves with fresh vegetables and having some to preserve for the winter time.

We also had air raid drills. The sirens would sound and we had to make sure all the lights were off or dark drapes were covering the windows. One day my mother had some kind of a deadline and she was very busy vacuuming when the sirens sounded. She continued to vacuum, thinking that it wouldn't be a problem. Soon we heard a knocking on the door and the neighborhood air raid warden told her the little light on the vacuum could be seen from the street. She would have to turn it off and not ever use it again during an air raid. We were very embarrassed that the warden had to knock on our door.

The day came when we sold the Model T. My father had to quit his job in the bank and go to work in a factory. The factories were being built outside the city. He needed a car to go to work so we bought a newer model, maybe a 1937 something and he had a higher gas ticket priority. We could only use it for his work and to go to the garden, and it had a key to start the engine.

Fall of 1962

by Joan Gomersall

I was a frequent visitor to the Cleveland airport when we lived in Berea in the 1960's. My husband traveled and I was always picking him up or dropping him off, a lot of the time with the kids in their PJs. One time he drove us to the airport to drop him off and then we all said goodbye at the gate and he boarded the plane. We usually waited until we saw the plane in the air and waved to it before we left the gate. But this time we were waiting, and the plane came back to the gate. The attendant asked, "Is Joan Gomersall here?" I said yes, a bit concerned, and he said your husband said to give you these – the car keys.

Another time in 1962, President Kennedy came to Cleveland to speak to the city fathers in down town Cleveland. I read about his visit in the newspapers – that he was coming and we also heard it on the news. They said he would be arriving at the Cleveland airport in early afternoon.

We lived close to the Cleveland airport in Berea, Ohio and I started thinking it was possible to go to the airport and see him deplane. I had four children. One was in morning kindergarten and so was Bobby a little boy the same age who lived across the street. Janice was four, Jennifer was two and Edson was only a few months old. I spoke with Mora, Bobby's mother, on the phone and we decided to go to the airport after we picked up Bobby and Susan from school. We packed some food, put my baby buggy in the station wagon, and piled in the little ones including Bobby's little brother and off we went.

There was no trouble driving into the airport and parking. I got the buggy out and had Edson in it and later put Jennifer in too with her feet in the front pocket. Now we each had only two kids in tow. We found out the best place to watch was on the roof of the terminal building. There were a lot of people there but we were not uncomfortable. We had a nice spot by the railing overlooking the tarmac. We did have a wait as the President was late, but we ate our food and kept the kids busy telling the older ones who we were going to see.

We noticed there was a squadron of motorcycle policemen waiting right below us. Finally the big magnificent Air Force One arrived and pulled up close to the building. The policemen formed a welcoming line from the door of the airplane and stood at attention. Then the door opened and this very tall man with the sun shining on his reddish hair, walked down. On TV his hair never looked that red. I remember he seemed a whole head taller than everyone else. As he walked through the line of policemen he stopped and shook everyone's hand. He walked to a microphone and gave a short speech and was put into a motorcade and left. We stayed there for another hour until he came back to the airport and watched him board Air Force One and the giant plane flew away with his giant cargo.

"Grandma, You're the One Who Turned Me Onto Harry Potter."

by Joan Gomersall

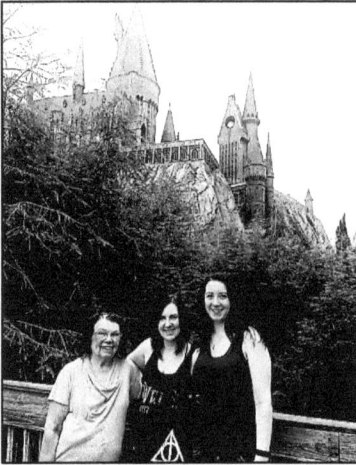

Joan with granddaughters, Erin and Colleen

"Remember when you bought me the first book and you read it yourself on the plane when you came to visit us on my birthday?"

"Yes and then you both read every book as soon as it came out even waiting until after midnight for some of the books."

"Remember on your 70th birthday party and you bought one for each of us as long as we didn't hide away from the party to read it."

This conversation went on at the Harry Potter theme park in Orlando, Florida. It was a marvelous way for us to spend time together and find all the magic that was in the Harry Potter stories.

Of course you needed a magic wand to make some things happen. Both granddaughters and my daughter bought special wands to suite their personalities. They had to be assessed by the wand maker as to different qualities and likes to get the right wand. These worked if you stood on special marked places on the sidewalk. They could make monsters move or roar or turn lights on or off a real interactive idea.

There was the train that transported Harry from London track 9 ¾ at Kings Cross station to the castle at Hogsmeade. Once in Hogsmeade, we took a ride to fly on broomsticks like the game of Quidditch. We were greeted by spiders and dragons and finally Harry led us out. We saw the big dragon on top of buildings still in Diagonal Alley that spit fire every 15 minutes.

The three of them took the rollercoaster rides but I opted out (I don't like them) but I could walk through to the end with the girls so I could see the dark spooky magical hallways. They were decorated with some pictures that talked. One was the Gringots Goblin Bank from the story.

The dining halls were just like the movie very dim and with old heavy furniture. The waiters represented people in the story. All were so friendly and helpful and so many costumed personnel were everywhere, especially in The Leaky Caldron where we ate our first dinner. The next night we ate at the Three Broomsticks restaurant.

We did some shopping in Diagonal Alley's quaint shops. Anything that was in the book or the movie was there, like monsters, owls, candy, clothing, the robes the students wore, the ties, tee shirts, scarfs, wallets like the one I bought, four days' worth of fun in the castles with steeples, towers and pointed roofs. On some roofs in Hogsmeade snow was evident adding to the mysteriousness of the evening, even though the temperature really was 90 degrees with 65 percent humidity.

At night the lights started coming on in the windows. The yellowish hue lent a quieter mystical atmosphere even though there were still many people. Maybe they were a little sluggish from walking around all day, but they were still with awe and excitement to see the next surprise.

Maybe it would be the butter beer. That was especially good. A pumpkin drink was a thirst quenching apple juice.

After four half days of happy sorcery, it was time to get our last taxi ride back to our hotel.

So Much for Rental Cars

by Joan Gomersall

I am sitting in a Nissan rental car in my driveway. It is 9:30 p.m. Wednesday night. It is already very dark and chilly and I am very tired. I just came from a lecture about goddesses. It was a series of several weeks and this was the last night. I was the chair person for the committee.

I had put my purse in the back seat as I usually do. Mostly because it is easier to do the same side of the car than to reach over to put it on the front passenger seat.

In the purse is my garage door opener. I was lucky enough to remember to take it out when I left my own car at the garage to be fixed after it was involved in an expensive fender bender.

Now I need to get out and open the back door to get the garage opener so I could put the car in my garage. I reach for the door handle to open my door on the driver's side and it doesn't open. I try again. It doesn't open. I keep trying. Then I start to explore other buttons and the trunk pops open. I don't know why. It is too dark to see much. I am just exploring. It is getting late and I have a mini panic. I don't have my cell phone with me and if I did it also would be in my purse in the back seat of the car. I could use a flashlight but I don't have one.

I am locked in my car and I don't know how to get out. I think of the panic button on my keys should I set it off and maybe my neighbors would hear it and come to my rescue and get me out of the car.

The street is dark. Everybody is probably in bed. I have been here at least 15 or 20 minutes. I think again and decide to use the button and wake up the whole neighborhood so I reach for the ignition and pull the keys out and I hear a sharp click. That is a good sign I try the cold door handle again and the door opens.

I quickly open the door like I am afraid it is only temporary and will lock again. The back door opens also. I can retrieve my purse with the garage door opener in it, and get back in the front seat and carefully pull into the garage.

Now I know I have to take the keys out of the ignition before I want to open the door. And maybe, next time, I will have my purse next to me in the front seat.

So much for rental cars!

Luanna K. Lynch Leisure

I had just finished my manuscript and was searching for a critique or writers' group. My husband, Herb, had recently been given a book by a client that she had written. I called asking if she knew of such a group. "Yes, I do," came her reply, "but first, I would like to meet you." So we arranged a visit.

After reading my manuscript, *Mystery at Lone Oak Ranch*, I was informed, "I think you might have something here," and recommended I go with her to a meeting of the National League of American Pen Women. Even though I felt very inadequate, I was accepted into this group of talented writers, artists and photographers. At one of the gatherings, I met Louise Webb. She handed me a slip of paper with her phone number and a message that read, "Call me."

Being somewhat curious, I called Louise and she invited me to her memoirs class. Not knowing what it was about I decided to attend anyway. At my first meeting I thought, "What am I doing here? I know nothing about memoirs." Once I listened to the stories of the members, I realized I had been writing my memoirs for years.

I felt right at home. We all had a story to tell. I found I could write and read to the class subjects I could not tell anyone else. It was a healing place, a shelter for tears, laughter and enjoyment. I have been attending Louise Webb's memoirs class since 2011 and always look forward to the next meeting. Thank you, Louise, for the invitation to your class. This has been one of the best decisions in my writing career.

I am a wife, mother and grandmother. I have now written and published three children's books and I am working on my fourth. At the same time, our class is working on *Best of Our Memoirs* book.

My website is:

www.LuannaLeisureBooks.com

Books may be purchased at:

LuLu.com and Amazon.com

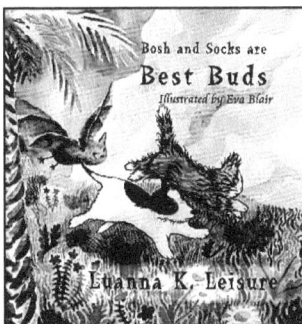

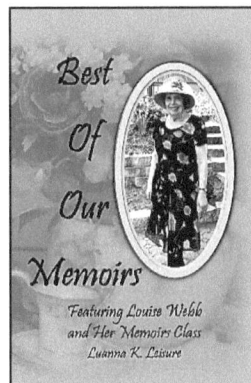

My Dog – My Friend
"Skippy"

by Luanna K. Lynch Leisure

I was about three years old when my sister, Barbara, who was about 23, brought us a tiny bundle of fur on four legs. His name was Skippy. I imagine Barbara named him, but I don't know for sure. My new friend arrived when I lived with my sister Sharyl, our parents and Grandpa Lynch in a big two story house surrounded by grape vineyards in Exeter, California.

Skippy grew up with me and lived well into my teen years. He had a long, shaggy, white and black coat. His tail was fluffy and curled upward.

I don't think I can truly express to those of you, who have not had a dog as a best friend or as a companion, how much doggie love these critters have for their human friends, and vice–a-versa, especially if you were together most every day for over thirteen years, as I was with Skippy.

I would call out, "Here Skippy, come here Skippy." He would come running and we would race through the grape vineyards together. Of course he would out run me and run circles around me. Sometimes I stopped to pick poppies as Skippy chased rabbits. On occasion he would come over and dig in the dirt close to where I was playing.

I loved all the feral kittens that were born in the vineyards and in the water tower, but Skippy didn't scratch me like they did, so he soon became my best friend. I can remember only once when I got mad at Skippy.

I was given a windup toy gorilla from my older brother, Bill. The gorilla was covered with fur and when I wound him up with the little metal key, he would walk around. It seemed like he moved his arms, but too many years have gone by and my memory has failed me as to what else he may have done, but I do remember playing with him all the time. My gorilla was the best toy I ever had. At least for that moment in time.

One day I caught Skippy playing with my gorilla, but I thought he was killing him. Skippy was tugging at the gorilla's fur and ripping it off. I remember screaming for mom and yelling, "Skippy is killing my gorilla."

By the time Mom found us, it was too late. In my mind, my gorilla was dead. He couldn't possible still be alive after Skippy skinned him.

My heart was broken. I cried and cried and couldn't even be consoled when Mom tried to glue the fur back on the tortured gorilla. I remember I couldn't stand to look at him half skinned with his fur in patches, and I couldn't stand Skippy. How could he do such a horrible thing to the poor little gorilla?

I eventually accepted Skippy back as my friend, but obviously to this day, I will not forget what he did.

Mom raised chickens for food and eggs. Skippy was smart and Mom taught him to look at her finger and follow it to where she was pointing. She would be pointing at a fat hen. When Mom said, "Get it, Skippy!" he would race over and gently grab the hen with his teeth and bring it back to her. Never did he puncture or hurt the chicken. The chickens would scatter when Skippy ran into the flock, and on rare occasions he would get the wrong one, but Mom would send him right back in to retrieve our dinner.

Skippy moved with us to Madera where we lived for about four or five years. Sister, Barbara and her husband, Rusty, lived a couple of houses away. She had a fenced area where Skippy could stay. I don't know why he had to stay there, but I would be with him as much as was allowed. When we moved to Visalia, to Park Street, Skippy came with us.

There were no leash laws so Skippy was allowed to roam free in our neighborhood, but he would always come back home. He would sleep on our front porch, up against the house, on an old blanket. One night we heard Skippy wildly barking. We all ran out of the house to see him pouncing on his blanket that was on fire. Someone had thrown a Molotov cocktail on Skippy and his blanket.

Daddy put out the fire but poor Skippy's feet were burned and his coat badly singed. We never found out who did it or why, but we gave Skippy credit for saving us and protecting the house from catching on fire.

Skippy, as many animals, seemed to sense when something was wrong. Grandpa Lynch was 87 and took seriously ill. As he walked out of the house down the sidewalk to get in the car, I will never forget what Skippy did. He laid down in front of Grandpa, put his head down and let out a sad moan. I remember it being very creepy and we had to make Skippy move out of the way. Grandpa never came back home. He passed away in the hospital.

Mom and Dad bought a house several blocks away on Stevenson Street. This was to be Skippy's last home.

He was my protector. If another dog came anywhere near me, he would chase them off. I would say, "sic'em, Skippy." Sometimes Skippy would get into bad fights with other dogs. He was a fierce fighter. One time when I came home from school, Skippy had a hind leg pulled up. He never again let it touch the ground. Daddy guessed he may have been hit by a car.

Skippy would go with me everywhere. He would scamper ahead of me to the grocery store about five blocks away. He would patiently wait for me at the door until I finished looking at the comic books and buying Hershey Bar.

The grocery store had a front and back door. On this one particular time, I went in the back door but when I left to go home, I took the front door. Later that evening it was dark out and I suddenly realized Skippy was missing. We looked all over and called for him and then I remembered he went to the store with me. Dad drove me to the store and I found Skippy curled up by the back door waiting for me. It had been hours and he hadn't budged. When he got up to hop in the car he could hardly move. Now that was true puppy love.

As Skippy grew to be an old man in dog years, there would be times he would stare at me, like he wanted to say something, and I would wonder, "What are you thinking, Skippy?"

It got to where he didn't feel like going on walks. His eyesight got bad and he didn't want to get up from his favorite spot on the side of the house. His long hairy coat now made him look more like an old, worn out rag mop. Dad said Skippy was in pain and we should take him to the vet to have him put to sleep. I knew what that meant. That was a polite way of saying that Skippy was going to die. I couldn't stand the thought of it, and I wouldn't let Dad. I would talk to Skippy, pet him and try to get him to eat. Nothing I did made him better.

After school one day he was gone. Dad said he died and I was so mad at my parents because I thought they took him to the veterinarian and I was mad because Skippy was dead. I asked what they did with him and they said they took him to where my brother lived and buried him out by the barn. I made them take me there. I looked at the place where they said they had put him to rest. It was the most unacceptable thing that had happened to me in my life.

I have had several dogs since then. I've even had a lot of cats. But none have been a companion, a fierce protector a best friend like my dog Skippy.

I Know Who I Am

by Luanna K. Lynch Leisure

As I began to type and gather my thoughts, I noticed my heart was beating faster and harder. Just the thought of putting this subject into words caused me anxiety, but it was also liberating and gave me joy. Why haven't I already written about this?

As a young child I was mischievous, joyful, full of laughter and fun, but as I got older, my joy diminished. I begin to notice I wasn't treated the same as my older siblings. This may have been my childish imagination. I know my parents did not show affection towards me or my sister, who was four years older.

Even though these childhood years were not the best of times, my personality was always positive and I had a way of bouncing back, thinking on the good rather than the bad. Cheerfulness has always been a part of me and many times I have not been able to contain it.

My birthdays should have been among my fondest memories, but I clearly remember never having any. I would turn another year older, but no one acknowledged the date. Since I was born on Christmas Eve, I was told one celebration was enough, so my birthday was ignored in favor of the Lord's. I remember one particular Christmas Eve dinner, when all the family was together. Mom pointed to a cake she had made, yet left undecorated and without Happy Birthday written on it, and she said this was my cake for my birthday. No singing, no acknowledgement—it was just there. I was confused and puzzled, but it made me happy I had a cake, and it was mine.

I have many childhood memories of Mom and Dad arguing, usually because Dad drank, and Mom hated his drinking. I never paid much attention to what they said, but their arguments would usually end with Mom repeating the same thing I had heard all my life. I always felt like part of their arguments were about me. When I was about 13 years old, another yelling match ensued, and I finally asked Mom, "What do you mean when you tell Daddy that you never knew there would be another little baby Lord Jesus born?"

Mom gasped and pushed Daddy into their bedroom. She slammed the door shut, but I could still hear her chewing him up one side and down the other. When she came out she said, "I will never say that again." Dad never said a word. He just sat down in his arm chair, but I still did not have an answer. I still did not understand, but Mom never said those words again.

Six years later at age 19, I was finalizing the details of my wedding. We had family visiting, and I remember lots of storytelling and laughter as they recalled their experiences from years gone by. I always enjoyed the stories, but my joy was crushed when my dad informed me that he was not going to walk me down the aisle or even attend my wedding. See, my dad was prejudiced, and my husband-to-be was half Portuguese and Roman Catholic. To top it all off, one time my fiancé kicked my dog when Dad happened to be watching. Dad said, "Any man who kicks a dog is of no account."

After the company left, I remember sitting on the floor by Dad's feet. All my tears and begging could not change his mind. I was so grieved and sad. Dad never did talk to me much, but as I sat there he looked down at me with his sparkling blue eyes and said, "You think that I don't love you, but I do." I was so shocked. I didn't even say I love you back. How could I? He had never told me he loved me before. I didn't know how to react.

A few minutes later, my fiancé came by and picked me up to go visit his grandparents. I wasn't even out of the car when someone came running over and told me to hurry back home because something was wrong with my dad.

When we drove up in front of my house the ambulance was already there, and Dad was on a gurney being put into the back of the ambulance.

Mom was crying and said, "He's gone." Family rushed back and we went to the hospital. He had a massive heart attack and could not be saved.

My thoughts at the time? He had just told me that he loved me, and – he was not going to attend my wedding. One thing for sure, he got what he wanted, he definitely was not going to attend my wedding.

About 15 years later, I mentioned to my sister about the times when Mom and Dad used to argue, and Mom would yell back the same saying to Daddy, "I never knew there would be another little baby Lord Jesus born." Throughout the years, this increasingly nagged at me.

Sister said, "It was because Daddy didn't think you were his." What a shocker. Why didn't I understand that before? It was like a floodlight illuminating the darkness in my mind. Her reply answered so many questions about why I believed I was treated differently and perhaps why my birthday was ignored, but now the empty feeling about my paternity begin to plague me.

In 2007 National Geographic offered DNA testing to find a person's deep ancestral roots. DNA testing intrigued me, and I signed up. I even convinced one of my brothers to take the test. Then in 2012 I took the Family Finder DNA test through Familytree.com. I realized this test would prove if I was a full sibling to my brother or a half sibling. I pleaded with my brother again to take this second DNA test, but without telling him why. He just thought I was doing more genealogy research.

I submitted the samples and checked online every day for the DNA results. Finally the results were in. Oh, my heart! It was pounding like the beating on a bass drum, and I felt like I couldn't breathe. I clicked on the results and there I was at the top of the list. I was a full sibling to my brother. I cried so hard I was sobbing.

The anguish—the heart ache—the stupidity of what a parent can put a child through. I wanted to dig daddy up and shake my finger at him and tell him off.

But, I have also discovered that I am the only child for whom Daddy bought a car. He gave it to me when I was a sophomore in high school. He said it wasn't mine, but I could drive it. I knew better. I knew it was mine. Just a few years ago I found out that Dad never told any of my siblings that he loved them. I was the only one. He told me in a backhanded way, "You think that I don't love you, but I do." I find this acceptable.

So – I am into genealogy and DNA testing because it has not only helped others solve parental mysteries, but it has also helped me. And now – finally – after a lifetime – I do know who I am.

I Believe In Miracles

by Luanna K. Lynch Leisure

Several near disasters events have happened to me over the years. The following are a few and are not necessarily in chronological order.

I was a single mom, traveling with some friends on the way to Disneyland. I was driving on interstate five, getting close to Anaheim. My son, Jimmy, was in the front passenger seat, daughter, Tracy, her friend, Julie and my son, Tommy were in the back. Our friends were in the car ahead of us. No cell phones at the time, but we did have CBs to chat back and forth or let each other know when it was time for a potty break. Our friend, Mike, was goofing around on his CB saying a bunch of nonsense stuff, just to get us to laugh and pass the time. Suddenly I noticed movement on the left side of my car window.

I instinctively turned my head and what I saw took my breath away. I started yelling, "Mike, look to your left." But crazy Mike was yakking away on the CB.

What did I see? A car had pulled up close beside me, going freeway speed, and a man was hanging out the passenger side window shirtless, completely bare skinned to his waist. I could see his mouth moving, yelling at me, but the horrifying sight was the gun in his hand pointing right at me. As he dangled out the car window yelling, he was pulling the trigger over and over. Then the driver sped up to our friends in front of us.

The crazy gunman was now even with Mike and his family. Finally, Mike stopped goofing around and I yelled into the CB, "Mike, look to your left."

I heard an expletive blurt out of the CB as the car sped on past Mike and took an off ramp.

We didn't know if the gunman was really trying to shoot us, maybe just a prank trying to scare us, but when we checked into our motel in Anaheim, one of the kids turned on the television. Again, I gasped for breath. The breaking news was about a gunman shooting at cars on the freeway. It showed cars with the windows shot out and mentioned children and adults in the hospital.

Did the gunman run out of bullets when he reached us? Did an angel have his finger in the barrel of the pistol? Was this a miracle that we were all saved from possible death? I can tell you what I did when I saw the news report. I fell on my knees and thanked my God.

This next incident sounds unbelievable. My teenage daughter was with me in the car and she knows this is true, we have talked about it many times over the years. Another person who was involved also knows this to be true. I wish I knew who she was so I could talk to her.

I had just dropped off Jimmy at school and was driving way too fast trying to get Tracy to school on time. I was driving a Dodge Maxi Van. It had bucket seats with the motor incased between them and a long bench seat right behind. Tommy was on the bench seat, but I didn't have him belted. In fact Tracy and I didn't have our seatbelts on either. It was before the law making it mandatory to buckle up. Tommy would often fall off the bench seat when I would barely tap on the breaks. If he did, he would either climb back up or just play on the floor.

As I was barreling down Linwood, a narrow street with a middle divider, a car suddenly pulled out in front of me and stalled. It seemed like I slammed on my breaks, but it was too late. Slow motion is what I felt and so did my daughter when we talked about it later. We were so close, I saw the woman's face frozen in fright. I remember so well how her mouth was wide open, she must have been screaming, and she threw her hands up to cover her eyes. Impact should have been in the next second. But I tell you the truth, our huge Maxi Van glided, (I want to say floated because that's what it felt like) but it glided smoothly, motionlessly, around the front of her car and I kept going on the other side of her at the same speed. Tracy and I said to each other, "What just happened?" We didn't move out of our seats. Tommy was still sitting on the bench seat and hadn't budged. I glanced back at the lady and her head was turned towards us as I zoomed on down Linwood Street. I wonder if she thought this was a miracle. I do.

Just a few years ago, my husband, Herb and I were visiting my family in Texas. Late one evening we were with my sister, Sharyl, and her husband, Bill, grocery shopping. Herb and Bill were putting the groceries in the back of the car and Sharyl and I were on the right side of the car talking when out of the shadows of the darkness two men approached us. They had on hoodies. One had his face covered with a bandana. The other had his shirt pulled up where you could only see his eyes. One moved in close to Sharyl. She clutched her purse to her chest and asked him, "What do you want?" She admitted later it was a silly thing to say, but she was startled by him being so close. The other man walked up close to me but brushed up against me and kept on walking. The other man did the same and they disappeared back into the darkness.

It was a puzzle to Sharyl and me as to what just happened. Were they just passing by us? Were they up to no good? Herb and Bill didn't notice them since they were busy with the groceries. Were the strangers bundled up and had their faces covered because they were cold? We were pretty naïve, because later that night the news was on and there were the two same banditos, seen on surveillance camera, robbing a convenience store with guns. Even after Herb and I got back to California, my sister called and said they were on the news again and still had not been apprehended.

These were situations that happened. No control over it. No request for any specific help on my part. It just happened.

But not this time.

Herb and I thought it to be a grand adventure to hike to Half Dome in Yosemite in the year we both turned 50. A few days before we started our trek, we were in Yosemite village getting our permits to go to the dome. Among the rules and regulations we were warned not to go up on the metal cables or be up on the dome if there was lightening. If we should get caught in a sudden storm, we should not have any metal hiking poles or anything metal on us.

Herb and I had hiked over halfway up the mountain on the way to the dome. We camped the night in the woods with the bears and critters. This will be another story for another time.

Early the next morning we continued the shorter trek to the top. I had reached exhaustion the day before and my restless sleep did not help me regain my strength. Complete exhaustion seized me right before ascending the cables up the dome. I told Herb to go ahead without me. I knew how much he wanted to conquer the dome. He went ahead and I threw myself on a huge bolder.

I didn't even care about the spiders and bugs traipsing all over it and on me. I laid there with my eyes closed for a long time. I finally began to feel a little better. From my vantage point on the bolder, I could see way down into the valley. It was beautiful. I finally crawled off and walked around. I was glad I rested and survived. The day was beautiful, perfect weather, not a cloud in the sky.

By this time, Herb had made it to the top and it seemed like enough time had gone by where he should be ready to start back down.

"But wait. What is that approaching?"

Off in the distance, approaching the dome was a small but angry thunder cloud. It was a dark, rumbling cloud. I thought, where there is thunder, there is lightening.

I kept watching the cloud get closer and closer. It was the oddest sight I had ever seen. It was the only cloud in the sky and it was headed straight for half dome. I was carrying a metal, military canteen so I threw it as far away as I could and I looked around for a low place in the terrain to duck.

I strained to look at the top of the dome to see if Herb was starting down. I saw him. He was far away but I could see the color of his shirt and he was the only person I saw making this trek alone. The cloud was getting closer. It appeared the cloud would reach Herb about the time as he would be on the cables.

I was in a panic. I didn't fall on my knees in prayer, I just talked to God and asked Him several times to please send the cloud back.

As Herb descended the cables I watched him disappear as he went behind part of the dome and some trees. I would glance at the cloud but I mostly focused on the trail where Herb would appear, and with great relief, he finally did. I asked him if he saw that angry cloud, as I pointed to where it should have been. He said he did, but when I looked to where I thought the cloud would be, the cloud was in the distance going opposite, back from where it came.

Why was I surprised? I shouldn't have been. I had experienced miraculous events before. Why should I have been so shocked when I asked and I received?

My husband says he believes that from my perspective I do believe these things happened in this way and that I believe them to be true. Were these happenings all just time and chance, as is Herb's perspective? Or were they miraculous events?

What is my philosophy? I believe there is another dimension. One we cannot see. I believe because I have experienced it. Unseen hands, forces, maneuvering, working, protecting, saving.

What do I believe? I believe in miracles.

Shanghaied in Shanghai

by Luanna K. Lynch Leisure

Seventeen years ago, in the fall of 1999, my husband Herb and I arrived in China with a tour group. Our visit just happened to coincide with the 50th year celebration of the People's Republic. There were gorgeous, red floral displays everywhere we went. My sensory receptors were on overload. Everything was different and at the time, I had no expectations, except one.

I am a collector of tea pots, cups and saucers. I have several of the Royal Albert, Bone China sets, which are made in England. My expectation was to bring home a beautiful tea set made in China. Herb didn't understand. He said, "You can buy the same thing at home." "No," I told him. "I have to buy it in China and bring it home."

Our first night was in Beijing where we stayed in the China Resources Hotel.

Of course I had to check out the hotel gift shop. And there it was. The first place we stayed I saw the perfect tea set. Delicate Bone China, gold trim around the detailed dark and light blue paint on white background. It was made just for me. I couldn't wait to tell Herb.

"No, we can't buy it now. We have two weeks of traveling around China by bus and plane, and there is no way we can carry a tea set in a big box and protect it from being broken. If you find something on the last day of our trip, we will figure out how to get it home."

I knew that was his final answer and I was sure he was thinking the chances of finding it on the last day would be slim and none. I asked someone in the gift shop, who spoke English and Chinese, to write down the name of the tea set and the manufacture. They wrote it in Chinese and everyone I showed it to, in all of our travels, said "Check in Shanghai, you will find it there." This was perfect, because Shanghai was the last leg of our trip.

But this did not stop me from searching for my prize at every shopping opportunity, which was many. Even the huge "Friendship Stores," our bus gravitated to, did not have my lovely tea set.

The rest of the hotels where we stayed – their gift shops were barren of any such delicate beauty.

After close to two weeks of seeing sites and searching, I was discouraged. I feared I missed my one and only opportunity to fulfill my expectation.

I will never forget the day we arrived in Shanghai. I first checked our hotel's gift shop for another disappointment, but more alarming, a convoy of Military trucks were bringing in armed soldiers for the final celebration and fireworks show for their 50th anniversary. An announcement was made that all Americans stay in the hotel and not go out for the fireworks. Even though he was warned, nothing I said would prevent Herb from going. He told me I could stay in the hotel, but, of course, I had to go along and protect him.

It was late and extremely dark out but being the only Caucasians, I can say we really stood out in the crowd, especially with my blond hair. I was standing behind Herb as he clicked photos when I was approached by an armed soldier. He spoke enough English that I understood he wanted to know where we were from. Herb wasn't paying any attention – still clicking photos.

"We are from the United States of America," I answered. For the rest of the evening the soldier kept his post next to us, either for our protection or to make sure we didn't do something illegal.

Whatever the reason, I felt safe with him there and we experienced a fireworks show that only the Chinese could do with such spectacular grandeur.

The night of fireworks was only leading up to our next and scarier adventure. Scarier for me – that is – not Herb.

It was our last day in Shanghai and I was still in search of my tea set. We were running out of time for me to find it. Our tour group was taken to lunch at a restaurant we had been to the day before – of which I was not pleased. I begged Herb to take me somewhere else. We heard there was a Hard Rock Café so we ditched our group and took off on our own in a Taxi.

After lunch, Herb saw a motor bike taxi and thought I might enjoy the experience of riding in one. Our driver was a robust lady. We sat in back in a tiny two seated cabin. I showed our driver the now flimsy slip of paper I had been carrying with the name of the tea set and manufacture. She nodded her head YES! I now had hope!

It was starting to rain and I was glad we were not walking. She drove up in front of a store which had a sign in English and Chinese. It said Chinaware Store. I was so excited. Maybe this store will have my prize!

My excitement faded to terror when Herb refused to pay the exorbitant fare our driver demanded. Herb offered her a lesser amount. Her answer was simple.

She put that bike in full speed doing donuts and wheelies. Skidding and sliding she traveled head on in the middle of traffic and pedestrians. She would stop suddenly with a jerk, turn around a frisk Herb from head to toe as he held tightly onto his wallet. When she couldn't get it, she sped off again, driving like a bat out of hell. I was screaming, "Pay her. We are going to get killed." Herb was laughing having a terrific time. He said, "It's better than a ride at Disneyland." The military and the police were still out everywhere and I was sure we were going to be arrested. This went on for several minutes with her driving antics, frisking Herb and me screaming. Finally Herb negotiated an amount she agreed with and she skidded to an abrupt halt in front of the Chinaware shop. Herb paid and I asked if I could take her picture. She seemed pleased and smiled. I later found out why she had such a smile. She had stolen my prescription glasses out of Herb's shirt pocket.

Shaken but not deterred, I was ready to go shopping. I felt like a kid in a candy store. I wanted to buy everything. Finally, there it was! How could this be! I had almost given up. It was the exact same tea set, and to Herb's joy, it was half the price of the one in the hotel.

We actually managed to get the tea set home without breaking a single, lovely piece. Herb had to cut the box to fit in one of our carryon bags. We kept the bag with us all the way home.

My purpose of this memoir was not to describe all my experiences and sites in China, which were more than I could possibly write is a short memoir, but rather to relate to you my quest and relentless search for that perfect tea set. I just had no idea that

to find it I would end up getting shanghaied by a motor bike taxi driver in Shanghai.

I'm Walking Kind of Wobbly Today
or
The Kiss That Knocked Me Off My Feet

by Luanna K. Lynch Leisure

I'm walking kind of wobbly today,
Not because of my favorite cabernet.

I walk in the house and I say, "Hey,
Hi my love, how was your day?"

In his recliner Herb is sitting,
Laptop open, he is reading.

I lean forward to give him a kiss,
He puckers up and we don't miss.

Just as we smooch my foot gets tangled,
The power cord! – my foot it has wrangled.

Backwards I fly and the computer goes too,
I land on my bum but I'm not through.

I keep on sliding – my back cracks with pain,
All I can say, "Is the computer okay?"

My sweet hubby replies, "For it I don't give a damn,
You're more important, here take may hand."

I open my eyes – the piano bench I've slid under,
I roll on my side, "Can I get up?" I wonder.

If I'm reading this I've made it to memoirs class,
And if you walk behind me just go ahead and pass.

I'm walking kind of wobbly today,
Someone – please pass me a glass of cabernet!

Memories of My Grandparents
or
Without Them I Would Not Be Me

by Luanna K. Lynch Leisure

Albert White and Vinnie Harsh White were my mother's parents. They had thirteen children. Eleven lived to be adults. They were always affectionate, and Grandpa would sometimes goose Grandma in front of God and everybody. Grandma might protest a little, but she never seemed to mind.

They were educated, had good handwriting and excellent verbal skills. Just not so educated when it came to birth control.

When I was about four, they babysat me. I was so excited the first time they took me to the grocery store. I piled the shopping cart high with packages of cookies. Not wanting to hurt my feelings or perhaps wanting to avoid a scene with me crying or begging, they reluctantly bought all the cookies. After they tattled to my mother, they made a rule. They would buy me one package of cookies each time we went to the store. Even though I knew the rule, I couldn't help but ask for more. Each time they said no, and I realized one package was better than none.

Grandpa White did not have a middle name. He was simply Albert White, but Grandma would call him "Ab." He was a tall, thin man, maybe 6 feet 2 inches. Most of the time he wore bib overalls. He had blue eyes, a fair complexion and brownish hair. He did not drink or smoke but I believe he did chew tobacco. He also enjoyed playing cards and gambled a little.

I remember Grandpa played a little game with the grandchildren and sold us lifesavers. We would have to ask our parents for a penny. He would take the penny, give us a lifesaver, then he would give the penny back to us. I found this to be a good deal. I kept the penny instead of giving it back to my dad, and, later, I bought

176

another lifesaver. After several deals Grandpa caught on and either cut me off or gave me the whole pack for one cent.

Grandpa White was also an excellent fiddle player. I loved to listen to him play. His music was fun and loud, and he would stomp his foot to keep the beat. I loved it so much, I would beg him to keep playing, and he usually tried to accommodate me until his arms gave out.

 Grandpa White lived to be 82 years old.

****

Grandma's full name was Vinnie Victoria Harsh. She was a short lady with dark hair, olive complexion and brown eyes. She had a big nose and a round face.

Grandma baked the best pies. Her walnut pie won first place at the Tulare County Fair. I have a picture of her holding a huge trophy. She loved to play cards and dice games like Yahtzee.

She was a member of the Helping-Hands Sewing Circle. It was a club for ladies who met in different women's homes to quilt, sew and mend. At one point Grandma was the secretary, and I have her notes recording one cent dues for each member and a gross proceeds of ten cents.

After Grandpa died and Grandma came to visit, I would bake homemade chocolate chip cookies for her. This was the least I could do after the many packages of cookies she bought me when I was little.

I enjoyed going out to lunch with grandma and my mom. I loved listing to them talk about family, and there was a lot of family to talk about. I was interested in a letter she showed me written by my great-grandfather who fought in the Civil War. He wrote about the stench of death and the rebels who came at him in waves of six deep. These stories first peaked my interest in our family history and genealogy when I was about eighteen. Grandma noticed my curiosity and sent me a copy of the letter.

 Grandma Harsh White lived to be 85 years old.

****

My father's parents were not at all like my mother's parents, even though I would consider them the "Salt of the Earth."

In other words, they were good people, willing to help those who could not help themselves, saying only good about others and worked hard.

My grandmother's full name was Effie Edith Idella Artivela Malinda Elizabeth Davis. (I have never heard the story of why she had so many names). She married my grandfather, William Henry Lynch. Grandma went by Effie and Grandpa was called Bill. They had five children.

I never knew my Grandma Effie. She died the year before I was born. I only know of her through stories and from a letter she wrote to my dad.

She was a petite lady, towering about 5ft. 3 in. tall with blue eyes, light brown hair and fair complexion. She may have been small, but she was mighty. She milked cows, churned butter, tilled the garden, raised chickens and worked the farm until she grew too ill.

Grandma chewed tobacco and smoked a pipe. I will repeat one story I was told about her, which is also a story about my practical joker of a dad.

Grandma smoked a clay pipe and used tobacco that her nephew harvested. One evening her son, my dad, took some powder out of a shotgun shell and put it in his mother's pipe. The next morning he waited until after breakfast for her to light her pipe. When she did, the gun power blew her pipe across the floor, then up and hit a window. She said, "My God, Willie Billie, what happened?" Apparently my dad thought it was a great joke. After that I was told she smoked a corncob pipe.

I'll include a letter Grandma wrote to my dad. It's sad, but also humorous. Dad and Mom had moved to California from their farm in Missouri, and Grandma wanted him to come back home, so she made her situation sound as bad as she could. In the letter she mentioned her daughter, Edith, who was born with Downs Syndrome. Something to realize, my Lynch grandparents were close to being illiterate. I will write the letter just as she wrote it, but I made the words more understandable. It took my sister and me several hours to translate her letter from backwoods hillbilly slang to something more legible and understandable. Also, my father's name was William Ethmer but he was called Ethmer.

Sep 28, 1945

Dear Son and Daughter,

How are all? Well I hope. This leaves us all in awful bad shape. I am getting worse and your dad can't hardly go. Ethmer, I am sorrow to write this to you. Edith has lost out. The doctor was here today. He said she was going through the change. She don't know much at times. She is giving us a sight of trouble.

Doc Hartley is dead. Bud is awful bad off. Ethmer, she is so bad.

Your dad can't see after your cows. Les said they was in the hay. I can't write no more. For God's sake do write and tell us when you are coming home. You don't know what we are going through with. You are needed. Your cows may die for water.

When you come be careful. Answer soon as you get this. Send it by air. Do this for my sake, Ethmer. We have to have somebody. Do let us know if you are going to come back.

From Mother to Ethmer.

This is about all I know of my Grandma Effie. She died five months after writing this letter. I wish I could have known her, heard her voice and listened to her backwoods language. She sounded like she was a real hoot!

Grandma Davis Lynch lived to be 73 years old.

****

I spent much of my childhood with Grandpa Lynch. I adored him. After Grandma died, Edith was put in a home. Grandpa couldn't take care of her or the farm without Grandma. He pulled up stakes, left the 120 acre farm to decay with no one living on it, and moved to California. He lived with us and sometimes with his daughter.

I remember much about Grandpa Lynch. He may have been about 5 foot 8 with blue eyes, medium light hair and a fair complexion. He had a big mustache that covered his top and bottom lips. It looked like he didn't have a mouth, it was just all hair. He wore khaki pants with suspenders and a long sleeved shirt. He also chewed tobacco and drank. My mom was on his case about his excessive drinking as much as she was on Dad's.

One time Grandpa was innocent. He drank some Welches Grape Juice that he found in the back of the refrigerator. It must have been in there for a very long time because it had fermented and poor grandpa got looped. Mom checked the grape juice and, sure enough, that's what made him drunk.

He had a cane that he had brought with him from Missouri which he had carved from a sassafras root. When Grandpa needed a new cane, he would walk through the woods on his property in Missouri until he found just the right sassafras sprout growing up out of the ground. It had to have a limb coming out of the side so he could make a handle. He would remove all the bark with his knife and whittle it into just the right shape. Sassafras wood will last forever as long as it is kept dry.

Like his son, Grandpa had an odd sense of humor. He would poke my sister and me with his cane if we slept in on Saturdays. He especially got a kick out of hooking our ankles with his cane, and he laughed as we flopped on the floor. Mostly, he used his cane to sturdy himself as he walked. Wherever grandpa went, he had his cane, his grey felt hat, a pocket knife and his pocket watch.

Grandpa Lynch would point to the stars at night and teach me the different constellations. He knew the seasons and the sign of the moon, and he studied the sky so we knew when to plant certain vegetables.

One thing he did, which was disgusting to me, was to slop a chunk of his chewing tobacco from his mouth onto my bee stings. The wad of tobacco only helped because I was thinking about that wet gob of gunk on my foot instead of the sting.

He made up for this by buying me a Hershey bar when we walked to the grocery store together. He was like my best friend, but, if I was his best friend, he sure didn't need enemies. When I was in the sixth grade I gave him the measles—not the three day measles either. He was one very sick grandpa.

The last time I saw Grandpa, Dad was taking him to the doctor. He had nose bleeds that wouldn't stop. He walked out of the house down our sidewalk with Dad, then my dog, Skippy, did a strange thing. He laid down in front of Grandpa, put his front paws out straight, crossed them, put his head down and moaned. I do believe Skippy sensed that Grandpa was not coming home.

Grandpa Lynch lived to be 87 years old.

****

My grandparents played important roles in my life. Each was a unique individual with a personality and ethnicity that they shared with me. I am a conglomeration of all those who came before me, going back to my grandparents, great grandparents and great great-grandparents. Back to the beginning of my ancestors.

Without them I would not be me.

Carol McFarlin

I was born in Los Angeles, California and attended UCLA. I am married with three children, two of whom live in California and one out of state.

I joined the Saratoga Senior Center and I enjoy playing bridge there. I also enjoy some of their other offerings. A few years ago I read about Louise Webb's Memoir Class in the monthly bulletin and decided to attend. I had seen Louise at the senior center and learned that she led the class.

It's been a few years now that I have been coming and listening to all the memoirs shared by the class members.

One of my favorite sessions at memoirs class is when we have a party and everyone brings some delicious snacks and a big cake.

Jim Oggerino

I first met Louise Webb about thirteen years ago when I started attending her memoirs class. My original reason for taking the class was because I had hit a wall in writing poetry and a good friend and author told me to write my memoirs to get past that wall. She also touted Louise's class. Some ten years or more later I'm still not really past the wall in poetry or fiction, but I have enjoyed writing my memoirs and hearing the memoirs of others in the class. Taking Louise's class has helped me to do something I may have never done on my own. It's a good thing.

I attended North Carolina State University graduating in 1960 with a BS in Nuclear Engineering. I didn't know it then but this was the prelude to 40 years of interesting and exciting work. Early employment was with Aerojet-General, where I worked six years on NERVA (Nuclear Engine for Rocket Vehicle Assist). This rocket was for a manned mission to Mars. I did nuclear core physics analysis, crew radiation dose calculations, and performed radiation effects testing on rocket nozzle pressure transducers.

From that project I joined the General Electric Nuclear Energy Division in 1968, where I started as an engineer in the Control and Instrumentation Department for commercial nuclear electric power plants.

183

This job morphed into International Technical Marketing. As Manager of Nuclear Component Sales in the Far East, I made frequent trips to Japan. The first Arab Oil Embargo caused the sale of nuclear material in Japan to plummet.

Next came Swiss Licensing. My family and I were transferred to Zurich, Switzerland from 1976 to 1979. I worked as a Liaison Engineer on the Kaiseraugst Nuclear Power Plant, which never got built. After 16 years I left General Electric.

My last long term employment was with the Electric Power Research Institute for another 16 years, where I held various positions, mostly in technology transfer at the division level and project management. I became the Manager of Technology Transfer for the institute. I retired in 1999.

Barbara has been my forever wife of 56 years. We have two children and two grandchildren. Our grandchildren are both honors students and athletes.

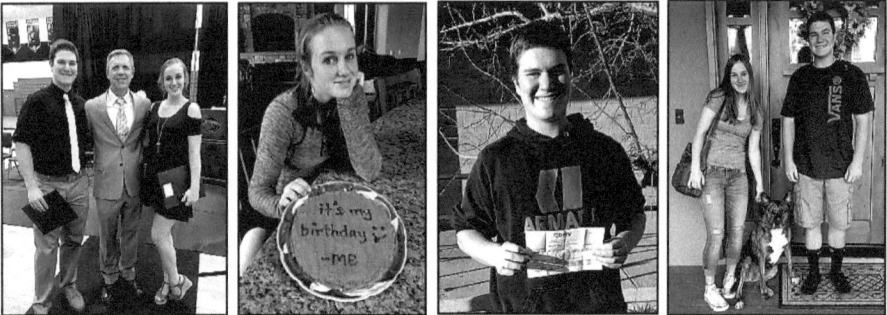

Grandchildren, Hannah and Alex
Left to Right: Scholastic Awards, Happy Birthday, Hannah. Congratulations, Alex, for passing driver's license test and first day of school 2016.

Along with writing poetry and my memoirs, I have enjoyed hobbies in volley ball, skiing, scuba diving, jogging and crew rowing. As age crept up, my hobbies became more sedate as a member of the Saratoga Rotary Club, and the Prize Winners Book Club, where we read mostly Pulitzer Prize and Booker Award books – the only way for an engineer to stay literate. . .

Having just past eighty years of age I can say that it has been a heck of a ride from an unheated, tenement apartment on the lower east side of New York City to a nice house in the Garden of Eden called Monterey, California. My dog and I travel for six minutes to go to the beach as often as possible. He loves the sand and water, and I love the waves, blue sky, and fog banks just off shore.

Christmas Choir 1943

by Jim Oggerino

We moved a lot when I was young. This was not a totally bad thing, because it now helps a failing memory to place events in time perspective. For example, I remember that I attended Our Lady Queen of Martyrs grammar school, on Arden Street in New York City, for the first second and third grades. Therefore, I was six, seven and eight years old respectively and I was in the Boys Choir at school. I remember being in the choir because one Christmas Eve I got to sing for my mother's mother.

My maternal grandmother's name was Gertrude Piffel. She was from Koenigsberg, Germany, which is on the northern coast of Germany on the Baltic Sea. Back then, people from this harsh land were called Prussians. I don't know when or why she emigrated from Germany to the United States, and whether she was already married to my grandfather. I knew that my grandfather did not live with her any more but the concept of divorce was beyond me at that age. No one spoke openly about divorce. She was a large woman, probably 250 pounds, and that could have made her scary. Her nose was rather large and her hair hung straight down from her head to her shoulders. Her dresses were like large sacks that were full of stuff. But despite her appearance, I seem to remember her with fondness. There was essentially no hugging and kissing in my family so I do not remember her in that way. However, most of the time I believe she was kind to me. Of course, grandma had a Prussian temper and when ignited you could get pretty badly singed.

One night, Grandma Gertrude had a massive stroke. I slept through the medics and the ambulance. In the morning she was just not there anymore. When I figured out she was missing I said, "Where's Grandma?" My mother said, "Grandma had a stroke and had to go to the hospital." I said, "What's a stroke?" My mother said, "It's a problem with the brain." I asked, "When is she coming home?" There was no answer to that.

Grandma's right side was totally paralyzed and at 250 pounds she did not receive any physical therapy in either of the county hospitals to which she was assigned. She survived like a vegetable for seven years. It was a long time before I knew what a terrible fate that was and when I found out I was sorry that she had not just died. In those days, you could not visit someone like that if you were under twelve years old, so I had to wait several years. When I finally did get to visit, I didn't really recognize her any more. I could be more graphic but it would serve no purpose.

Every once and a while when I begged everyone in the family for money for some silly reason she would slip me a quarter to spend as I wanted, and in those days that was a big treat. She would be sitting at the kitchen table in our railroad apartment on east 87ᵗʰ street, call me over and say, "Jimmy, I want you to have this. Go and have some fun." I don't remember ever seeing her go and have some fun. She would just sit at the table and talk to some of her cronies over coffee and cake (the slang for it at the time was a *kaffee klatch*), or she would just sit there with her leg shaking back and forth and stare into space. One time she caught me lifting the lids to the pots on the stove to see what smelled so good. She said, *"Was willst du, kleiner topf gekucher?"* Translated this means, "What do you want, you little pot peeker?" I rolled on the floor to *"Topf gekucher."* It just sounded funny. Another funny thing she said was *"Du bist ein böse boop!"* That means, "You are a bad little boy." She called me that in anger once, but I laughed so hard it became a joke between us. I was her, *"böse boop,"* her bad little boy. She'd see me and say, "Ach, hier ist mein böse boop," – Ah, here is my bad little boy.

Before she had the stroke, I remember the choir getting ready for Midnight Mass in 1943 or maybe 1944. We had a lot of choir practice to prepare for the big event - the birth of Christ. In those days the Mass and the hymns were still in Latin and it took a lot of time to master the arcane words. We not only had to remember the hymns, but at Midnight Mass the choir would sing the responses that the Alter Boys usually provided to the priest celebrating the Mass. There was "*Kyrie Eleison* (Lord Have mercy)," said three times, and responded to with "*Khriste Eleison* (Christ have mercy)," said three times, and followed again by three more "*Kyrie Eleisons.*" There was, "*Agnus Dei qui tollis peccata mundi* (Lamb of God take away the sins of the world)" with the response, "*Miserere nobus* (Have mercy on us)". There was the Our Father, "*Pater noster, qui es in caelis…*" which we all said together, and then "*Dominus Vobiscum…*(The Lord go with you)" which we kids always made fun of by saying "Dominoes, two bits and up," responded to with "*Et cum spiritu tuo* (and with your spirit)."

For many years in my childhood these words were soothing to me. They came from a ritual of peace and love. Years later in a Catholic high school in the Bronx, after getting out of detention late one day, I passed the school auditorium and about fifty Xaverian Brother teachers were singing some medieval chants in Latin. I just sat on the floor outside the auditorium and listened. I don't think I had ever heard anything so beautiful in my life – up to that time anyway.

After practicing for the choir so much I asked my grandmother, "Please grandma, please come up to our house and come to church for Midnight Mass and hear me sing in the choir." I don't remember how she accepted, but it happened. We were all going to go to Midnight Mass, my mother, my father, and grandma.

Christmas Eve finally came for me and I had to go to the church early and dress for the choir. I remember being so excited because my grandmother was coming to church just to hear me sing. We dressed in long red cassocks, like the priests wear. These had a million buttons in the front. Over the red "dress," we wore a white, frilly over-blouse. The choir sang from a loft in the rear of the church. We had a great view of the congregation and the altar. The altar was decorated with a red sash like a long dining room tablecloth, and there were scads of flowers to each side of the Tabernacle. All the gold accouterments were out: the chalice, the tall crucifix, the incense burner, etc. The lights were turned up high augmenting the dozens of candles giving everything some extra energy. People started coming in well before Mass started, and my grandmother was one of them. She sat pretty far forward. I don't know if she saw me, but I could see her and when I was singing I made believe she could hear just me.

The Mass itself was long and very detailed. There was an initial processional by several priests and the altar boys, where they went up and down the aisles. Incense was burned in the incense burner, which was swung many times to spread the fumes. The bells were rung at different times during the Mass, and of course the soprano boys choir was magnificent when singing the hymns or responding to the priest's chants. I think we did pretty well that night. I am sure the Mass took way more than the usual hour, but that was okay. I got to stay up late and sing to my grandmother, and I got to participate in a very special and moving ritual. When I got home I even got to open one of my Christmas presents.

As a closing thought to this story about things that I had long forgotten, this activity in my youth may be the reason I get a little angry when I see Christ taken out of Christmas and replaced with a big "X", and also why I get upset when I see stories about poor treatment of the elderly.

Closing Down 87th Street

by Jim Oggerino

We once lived in a ground floor apartment at 353 East 87th Street in New York City. So many of our clan lived there on and off over the years that I jokingly refer to this apartment as the "Oggerino compound," like the Kennedy's have their compound. Except this compound was a $28 a month, unheated, five-room "railroad" apartment (so named because all the rooms were in a line like railroad cars). But it at least had hot, running water.

Grandma Piffle (my mom's mom) originally rented the place, probably with her son, who was my wacky Uncle Eddy. In 1944, when I was eight years old, my dad went off to the Marine Corps and World War II, and my mother, my sister Jean, and I lived at the compound with Grandma and Uncle Eddy, who was already home from World War II with a hundred percent medical disability from the Army. For a short time my mother's sister Elsie, and her husband Herbert, from Red Hill, South Carolina, lived with us until they moved back to South Carolina, where they lived in a clapboard house with an outhouse for a bathroom, and a well with a bucket winch for water.

Somewhere in there, maybe in 1946, Grandma had a massive stroke and lived bedridden and paralyzed on her left side for seven years in a county run facility on Long Island. Then, it was just Mom, Jean, Uncle Eddy and me at the compound. Between 1947 and 1949, Eddy lived alone while the rest of us lived in Jacksonville, North Carolina with Dad for two years. But in 1949 we headed back to 87th Street again. This was when my dad decided to make his way in the civilian world in New York City, instead of Jacksonville. Because dad didn't know how to be a civilian he re-enlisted back into the Marine Corps in 1951, and Mom, Jean, Uncle Eddy and I were on our own again at the compound. At this point, I can imagine dear reader that all this shifting around in time and space is hard to keep up with. It was hard to live it and it's making me dizzy just writing about it.

In the spring of 1953, when I was in my junior year of high school at Cardinal Hayes in the Bronx, the Marine Corps shipped my father to the Great Lakes Navel Training Station in Waukegan, Illinois (Jack Benny's birthplace) to study Journalism. He was being trained as a Marine Corps Combat Correspondent, a profession he later put to use in Viet Nam as the oldest Marine "in country." We found out that after his schooling he was going to be stationed at Camp LeJeune, North Carolina, and we thought we would be joining him in North Carolina after his graduation. But Dad was feeling very lonely in Waukegan so in early to mid-summer of 1953 we decided to finally turn the "railroad" apartment back to its actual owner.

Wow, we were really going to close down the 87th Street compound. It seemed unbelievable. I had so many friends and memories in that part of the world at that time, leaving and starting over yet again was not the best news I ever got. Moreover, the minutia of closing down 87th Street and getting me to Waukegan didn't play out too well.

Eddy's heart was very weak from the Malaria that he'd gotten in New Zealand or Australia, and he was not physically able to take care of himself. So the first thing we had to do was make arrangements for him. Herbert and Elsie agreed to take him in, in South Carolina. In 1953 the airlines were still using propeller planes, and I guess the Eastern Airlines flight from New York's LaGuardia Airport to Columbia, South Carolina was quite devastating to Eddy's system. We were informed that he nearly died on takeoff and the stewardesses had a heck of a ride giving him oxygen along the way. He was taken off the plane to an ambulance. Initially he survived the trip and took to living in the country, but within three months he died from a heart attack.

After Eddy was gone, we packed as much as we could in boxes provided by the Marine Corps contracted movers. Then Mom and Jean left for Waukegan about a day or two before the movers got to the compound. I'm not sure what the logic was in doing it this way, but I think it had to do with the urgency that dad wanted someone in Waukegan.

The forty-eight hour period between my mother and Jean's departure and my departure were perhaps some of the toughest in my life to that point. Nothing outrageously serious happened, but issues of loss, fear, anxiety, trust and charity sure popped up. At the time I was a big strapping kid, but I was quite naïve and I had a learning curve on life coming up. This all happened more than 50 years ago, so some of it is hazy. But the series of events that happened were emotionally traumatic and in one case, physically life changing.

Typically, in a move by professional movers (and I use the term lightly), you get packed one day and loaded the next. The day after Mom and Jean left for Illinois, two packers showed up in the morning. Based on moves that I made later in life, my recollection of these packers is that they fit the mold. They did not seem to be college educated and bright eyed and bushy tailed. They seemed more like the expression, "rode hard and put away wet." Even as a naïve seventeen year old I could tell that these were not the cream of the crop. Still, that did not allay my actions in being Mr. Helpful. After all, I was a big kid full of nervous energy. I remember running around all day helping the packers pack. I don't remember eating or taking the time to eat, but I do remember that I was almost passing out hungry by the time they left. I finally heated two cans of Campbell's tomato soup and scoffed that down. I don't remember that night except that the only thing in the apartment not ready to move was my bed, and that would be taken down the next morning.

The next day, a truck larger than any I had ever seen before showed up outside the apartment house and two more of God's less than perfect creatures showed up to load the truck.

It was on this day that my naiveté really blossomed. I ran my strong little ass off all day long helping to carry boxes and furniture out to the truck. Sometime during the day I noticed that something had changed. There was silence when before there were sounds from my Hallicrafter radio. It was a regular radio, but it had short-range and long-range bands and I could get stations from almost all over the world. I had worked an entire summer delivering orders for a butcher the year before so that I could buy that radio. I guess the moving men decided it should be packed and not make the manifest, which means they stole it. I asked them about it and they talked about some guy that had come in the apartment while they were doing stuff and he probably took it. I must have seemed like such a dunce to them. I searched their truck as best I could but I never saw that radio again and I was very upset and sad. Based on the amount of things stolen during moves I made later in life, I think stealing must be in the DNA of packers and loaders. In fact, when we finally got our stuff in North Carolina about three months later I found out that a coin collection that I had was also stolen. It contained an 1837 quarter in pretty good shape, but the collection was in a box that allowed the coins to rattle – pure music to a mover's ears. The box was in a carton we had packed ourselves, but that was no deterrent.

As an aside here let me say that in 1979, when we moved back to the U.S. from Switzerland, an entire collection of my wife's Hermes scarves disappeared. The Italian packers that did that job were not as honest as we thought, since nothing in Switzerland is ever stolen. It seems that if you have valuable stuff, and you have to move, it is better to box your own boxes beforehand and make sure what you packed does not rattle.

When the movers left I was sad, hungry and exhausted, but I had a flight to catch. My folks had left me with an airline ticket, and some money – enough to get a taxi out to LaGuardia Airport and a little extra. I had never before been to an airport much less flown on a plane. To say that I was stressed and that my insecurities had kicked in was a severe understatement. When I got to the airport with my footlocker, my only luggage, I was able to check it at the counter of the airline I was supposed to fly with. I say, "… supposed to fly," because for some reason the plane was not going anywhere, or it was not anywhere, or something. Moreover, in my parents need to save some money my airline ticket was purchased on a non-scheduled airline. The scheduled airlines included American, Eastern, United, etc. Non-scheduled airlines worked differently – they flew once in a while when the flight was full. I was able to make a collect call to my folks but I don't remember the results of that except that I was stuck in New York with essentially no money and nowhere to sleep. Moreover, I found much to my dismay that, except for some change, I had lost the only money I had, which was a $20 bill and that was worth a lot in those days. It was about six o'clock. By talking to some really very nice people that worked for the airlines I found out that there was a late scheduled flight (probably on United) to Chicago but I needed money for my ticket. I decided to leave my footlocker checked and took a five or ten-cent subway ride back to the City. I was going to try and borrow the money I needed for the extra ticket from one of my friends. The subway trip was from LaGuardia Airport to Grand Central Station, with a change to the Lexington Avenue IRT, and an express ride from 42nd street to 86th street. From there it was a four block walk to my friend Martin's apartment house (that his family owned), just a few doors away from the one in which the compound was located.

The trip took at least an hour and I was running out of time. I got to my old neighborhood, went to Martin's house and told him and his parents my plight. I swore on my mother and all that was holy that if they loaned me the money I would send if back via telegram the next day. They gave me the money but I remember it as being a close call—they didn't just hand it to me. I quickly went back to the subway, and back to LaGuardia, and back to the non-scheduled airline counter to get my footlocker, so I could recheck it when I bought my new ticket. When I got to the baggage area, the non-scheduled airline counter was closed for the night and my footlocker was sitting proudly on a shelf behind a steel security gate. No one could open the gate so I had to leave my footlocker, as the baggage area was not going to open until the next morning.

I went somehow over to the United Airlines counter (at least I think it was) and bought my new ticket. As I was getting my ticket I told the "angel" behind the counter my story of having to borrow the money to fly, and losing my spending money, and having been back and forth between Manhattan and the airport twice in the last four hours, and the fact that I was starving and that I would not be able to eat until the next day. And you know what she did? She gave me an airline chit to go to the airport restaurant and get a meal. That chit translated into two hamburgers and a malted milk shake – probably the closest thing to manna from heaven that I ever had up to that point in my life. After a short wait, and another collect call to my folks to tell them on which flight I would arrive and when, I was able to board the plane for Chicago. I didn't know it then, but there was a lot more in store for me, some of it not good.

My flight left around eleven o'clock that night. Considering that in 1953 planes were still propeller driven I estimate it was a 3-hour flight for the thousand miles to Chicago, and since we would gain an hour by time zone change I assume we got in about one o'clock in the morning. I was so wired from the events of the day and being on my first flight I don't think I sat in my seat more than ten minutes of the entire flight. I walked the aisle, and stood in the back and talked with the flight attendants (back then they were stewardesses) when they would talk with me. It was a very long flight.

When I landed, my mother met me. We greeted each other as usual with a smile and a hello. Our family was not much for hugging, but that does not mean we did not care for each other. For some reason we needed or wanted to go to the non-scheduled airline. I think it was to leave word what to do with my footlocker when it arrived later in the day. Because it was a non-scheduled airline it was in a different terminal. Neither of us were familiar with airports and we started out walking to the other terminal. It turned out to be about a mile away, so there we were about two-o'clock in the morning walking along a steel fence in the dark for about a mile or so – the length of the runway. Naturally, when we got there the place was closed. It is absolutely amazing the stuff you can do when you don't know what to do, and you don't know that you don't know. Luckily, we were able to get a bus to the train that would take us from downtown Chicago to Waukegan, a distance of some 20 to 40 miles. While we were waiting for the elevated train (I think it was called the Skokie loop) the bars were closing and the drunks were out, and a couple of them decided to have a real punch out just below where we were standing on the train station platform. One of them may have had a knife. Welcome to Chicago.

By the time we got to Waukegan, I had been up for almost 24 hours – a first for me. I had helped to load a moving truck, been through some rather hectic stress, had eaten minimal food (remember I weighed about 200 pounds, none of which was fat), and I was totally exhausted. I do recollect that we got home about four o'clock in the morning and dad did not get up to greet me as he was sleeping so that he would have a clear head for class in the morning - that is why mom had to make the trip. I knew that I had to get up in a few hours to call the airlines about my footlocker and send the money back to Martin and his family via Western Union – that also would be a first for me. I guess I slept until about ten o'clock. I don't remember doing the Western Union thing but I do remember calling the airline and they said they would not be responsible for my stuff if I did not get it by the next day, so I had to learn how to get the train back to the City, get the bus to the airport, and make the return trip.

I went out for a while during the day and I began to meet the neighborhood kids about my age. To be honest, I don't remember a single one of them specifically, but I do remember they were pretty nice. They told me that they were going to have a softball game on Sunday morning (the next day) and that I should join in. Finally, I felt that some semblance of normality was coming back into my life – but that was not to be. On Sunday morning we went to the schoolyard to play our game of softball. They stuck me out in left field, because I said I was pretty fast and I could throw a ball.

Let me give you another aside here regarding being pretty fast. This is only to highlight what was about to happen. I had played football for Cardinal Hayes High School, where a team of 55 guys was culled out of a student body of over 3,000 boys. It was a tough, big team. We had two undefeated seasons. Each evening after two hours of head to head practice, we would do wind sprints, which meant that we would sprint a hundred yards about fifteen to twenty times. Because I worked for a butcher, delivering orders with a balloon tire bike all around mid-town Manhattan, I had very strong, large thighs and could run very fast. On the 55 man squad I was always first or second in all the sprints – usually first. After wind sprints I would see black stars on the way into the locker room, but it was always a good feeling to be so fast and to excel. Up to that point in my life I don't remember excelling at anything else.

So, here I am in the outfield on the school grounds in Waukegan, grounds that I was not familiar with, playing with a group of new peers I wanted to impress so I would be, "one of the boys." Someone hit a long fly ball to my position, but it was way over my head. I took off as fast as I could after the ball. I remember thinking, "Man your flying." Just as the ball came down into my glove I hit the pipe-iron fence that surrounded the school grounds. You know the type of fence I mean. There are two horizontal pipes, about two and a half inches in diameter, one shin high and the other thigh high off the ground. I literally flipped end over end over the fence, stood up, threw the ball in to someone else, and passed out. The next thing I knew I was being taken to the Navy doctors at the Great Lakes Naval Training Station Hospital. They put nineteen stitches in my right shin and taped my right thigh up because it was severely contused. They probably gave me aspirin or aspirin with codeine and sent me home.

About four hours later, I caught the train to Chicago, so I could go to the airport to get the footlocker that had all my clothes and other stuff that a teenage boy collects. I guess dad really was too busy to help. Except for being in a substantial amount of pain, and having to carry my footlocker to the bus station from the terminal, and stand for about an hour on the bus to get the train, the trip was uneventful.

During the course of that summer I got to know quite a few of the guys and girls at the high school. The plan was that I would attend the school for about two or three weeks and then, when dad graduated from his school, we would leave for North Carolina. I did make friends, and I did go to dances, and I did do a bunch of stupid stuff, like the other teenage boys. I had thought that the guys on the New York teams were tough, but these mid-western teenagers were a step up. They looked at playing football as a means of getting in shape for their real sport – wrestling. When I say they were tough, I mean physically. My memories of the "kids," in Waukegan were that they were really nice and I got to see a side of being a teenager that I had not seen in New York.

I did play in one or two football games at the beginning of the season, and then we got word that my Uncle Eddy had died. He had been doing very well after his almost fatal flight, but then he got a blood clot to the brain and died in his sister's arms. It was such a waste of a life. Eddy had been a shy boy with a heart murmur that was taken into the Army during wartime and would not have been inducted at any other time. He got malaria overseas and that weakened his heart totally. To my knowledge he had never had a girlfriend and never been out of New York City except for the Army. It's almost as if he never was. He always treated me kindly, and I guess I was like the son or brother he never had. He bought me my first bicycle – a Schwinn – and he took me to the movies and vaudeville shows. These were his prime source of entertainment and activity. He was a little wacky, but when I call him, "Wacky Uncle Eddy," I do it with a great amount of affection.

When my Dad applied for compassionate leave to South Carolina, with only a few days of Journalism school left, the Marine Corps decided to speed up his graduation from Great Lakes and told him to go to Camp LeJeune, North Carolina after going to South Carolina. Our prompt departure from Waukegan caused me to have to say goodbye rather quickly to the many friends I had met that summer, and when it came time to say goodbye to my teammates in the locker room we actually cried. I had really bonded with these guys and they had bonded with me. So about a week into the school year our family drove to South Carolina and Uncle Eddy's funereal. I had met a girl in Waukegan who was a little older. It was exciting to walk a nineteen-year-old girl home from work about 11 O'clock every night as a sort of bodyguard and friend. When we got to her house we would kiss a little and she would go inside. I have to sadly report that she left my virginity intact, and in the end I could see how I was being used, but it was a different sort of thing for me – exciting, frustrating and neat.

I have one last thing to report about really closing 87th Street down. Above, I mentioned a life-changing event. It turns out that while I was junior at Cardinal Hayes High School, part of what I did on the football team was to kick off during our games and kick field goals. Because of my strong legs and an affinity for kicking, I could kick off sixty-five yards (five yards into the end zone) with a hang time of over four seconds. If you are not familiar with football, being able to do that, at that time, was professional football quality stuff. Being fast, and having a head start when kicking the ball off, I often made the downfield tackle on the kickoff. I was looking forward to a college career and perhaps a professional football career with this fairly decent talent. It turns out that the blow to my thigh when I ran into the pipe iron fence that first day in Waukegan, caused certain muscles in my thigh to atrophy. After I healed I just didn't have the snap in my leg to kick pro-like anymore. I was still able to run fast, but I could not do the thing I was best at. It was a dreadful loss.

So, in the end we really shut more down then 87th Street. The apartment was gone, Uncle Eddy was gone, my Hallicrafter radio and coin collection were gone, my Waukegan friends were gone, and my potential career as a kicker was gone. More than 50 years later, I'm not sure yet if I know what to think of it all. Afterwards, it was on to Camp LeJeune High School with new friends, and new teammates, and new classes.

Mr. Echeberry

by Jim Oggerino

I'm sixty-six now. There are two reasons I know this. One is the number of physical infirmities I am beginning to experience and the other is that I seem to remember those things that happened decades ago better than I remember the things that happened two weeks ago. Maybe this latter phenomenon can be categorized as one of the infirmities. But this story is not about me. This story, if I can capture it, is about a Basque shepherd named Mr. Echeberry.

In his book, "Travels with Charlie," after spending an evening talking and drinking with a group of French Canadian migrant potato harvesters in Aroostook County, Maine, John Steinbeck writes, "There are times that one treasures for all one's life and such times are burned clearly and sharply on the material of total recall." I believe this to be an accurate statement, although I struggle at times with clear and total recall.

In late 1967, the company I worked for, Aerojet-General, transferred me from Sacramento, California to San Ramon, California, a move of about ninety miles. We rented a house in Dublin, California because it was only a four mile shot up the freeway to my work, and because it was all I could afford emotionally. In retrospect, the house and the town were dreadful. The house was an inexpensive tract home with a slab floor and everything in the house was inexpensive and tacky. Its only saving grace was that it was only a half-block from the grammar school with no streets to cross. The town of Dublin sits at the confluence of two mountain ranges. These are not very high mountains but mountains nonetheless. They form a natural funnel that directs the off shore wind from San Francisco Bay (about 40 miles away) down to Dublin. Every day, at a given time in the afternoon, the wind is more terrible then the rest of the day. All this wind pushed an awful lot of grit under the front door. My wife was pretty unhappy at this time but I was too busy, or too dense, to notice. Actually, she was busy too because my son Christopher was six years old and my daughter Anne was four.

My wife and I and the kids used to take exploratory rides on the weekends. After all, it does take a pioneering spirit to leave ones families behind on the east coast and move to the west coast. We would try to find interesting places to visit, and it was not too hard because California in the sixties was a much different State, and there were many more "wild" places to visit without a long drive. On this Sunday we had gone only two or three miles north on what is now I-680 when we saw, in the fields to the east, a man and two sheep dogs herding a couple of hundred sheep. My wife said, "Let's go closer and watch that man and his dogs." I agreed this was worth watching and got off at the next exit ramp. We made our way over to the fence where the man had parked his trailer, or someone had parked it for him because there was no car around. His trailer was one of those that could hold maybe two people and had a curved rear end with a small window in the curve. It looked more like an apostrophe then a place to live. The shepherding action was taking place about fifty yards away, but we could hear the man whistling and see him giving arm signals. At each sound or wave, the two dogs, black and white Australian Sheppards, would zig and zag and jump over each other, and nip and bark at the sheep to get them just where the man wanted them. But the sheep didn't much like it and made that known with a lot of loud "baaahs" as they scurried along. We watched with joy. It was not an everyday occurrence to see such a thing and I could tell by the smiles on the children's faces that they were really enjoying it. After a while the man and his dogs headed back to the trailer. As he approached we could see that he was not a young man. In fact, he was older then I am now or at least looked older. His face was grizzled from years in the sun and wind and outdoors. He wore dark dress pants and an old white dress shirt. He might have weighed a hundred and thirty pounds. He didn't have many teeth left, but he had a pleasant smile. That first day we just said our hellos and asked him if he minded our watching him. His English was only slightly better than our Basque so there was a lot of grunting and pointing going on. But it was clear that he enjoyed our visit, especially our children to whom he deferred, and it was clear that we were not causing him any distress. It was not until many years later, after I had suffered periods of terrible loneliness that I could begin to imagine how lonely he might have been. Maybe he was calm in a lonely life because that day he showed us a pen where he kept an injured lamb and its mother. Maybe his sheep were his surrogate family and it kept him from being lonely. He also showed us a small, straight-backed, wooden chair under a tree. He mimed to us that he rested by sitting in that chair and leaning against the tree. It's almost odd in today's helter-skelter society to think that a man could find peace sitting in a chair leaning against a tree.

I don't remember if we went in his trailer that first day, but we told him we would come back the following week. My wife is both an extremely competent nurse and a great cook, which I suspect is not a usual combination of talents. She felt that Mr. Echeberry might not be feeling well and could use some real nourishment, so she cooked a big dish of Lasagna for our next visit, which took place on the following Sunday. When he saw us, Mr. Echeberry immediately came over to the fence. My wife offered him the food and he reluctantly accepted it. He invited us into the trailer. It was a tight fit for the five of us but we squeezed around the little table. He was profuse and animated in his thanks for the food, but in his Old World way we had put him on the spot for he had nothing to give in return. Finally, he solved the dilemma. He brought out one of those large Hershey bars, the one that weighs about a pound, and offered it to Chris and Anne. He also gave them each a shiny quarter, which they kept for years afterwards. Although we thought it might tax him financially to give the candy and money away, we accepted his gift because he needed us to accept. During the animated conversation that ensued, mostly between the children and my wife, because Mr. Echeberry was a man and my wife and children complemented that fact, we found out that he had recently been in the hospital for an extended stay because of a large tumor they had removed from his abdomen. He said that he was fine, but even I could see that he was not fine, and of course my wife reconfirmed her instant diagnosis from the week before. We must have stayed and talked and laughed for an hour or two. The communication gap got smaller and the understanding got much better. Finally though, we had to go because it was time to go. I think we went back to visit once more, and then one day the sheep and the chair and the trailer and Mr. Echeberry and his dogs were gone. We knew from our previous conversations that he had probably been moved up and over the hills to the east, but we had no way to get there nor did we know where to go. We never saw him again.

Thirty-five years ago, the land between Dublin and San Ramon was just that - open range. It was part of the Bishop Ranch and it had nothing on it but California oak trees, scrub grass and wild mustard plants which covered the fields with bright yellow in the spring. Now, one is hard pressed to see any natural dirt in that area. It is either covered with roads or the commercial buildings to which the roads lead, or plants and trees hauled in to make the nice landscapes around the buildings. If you are driving on I-680 and you are a mile or two south of Crow Canyon Road or San Ramon Boulevard (which was not there at the time) you will see a very large green-metal and glass building complex, with a sign out front that says Bishop Ranch Business Park. When I drive past that spot I look east and see a grizzled Basque shepherd named Mr. Echeberry, leaning against an oak tree in his hard back chair, whistling at his dogs and watching them work the sheep.

I Miss Me

by Jim Oggerino

Lately, I've found myself feeling nostalgic about the old me, or perhaps better said, the former me. This feeling pervades almost every aspect of my being; intellectual, emotional, and physical. I feel a need to get more in touch with these feelings and a memoir seems the best way to do that. I'll start with the physical, because that may be the easiest to recall. In recollections of my physical or athletic self, I seem to see it all as a long video with a sub-orbital trajectory - a great growth in the upward direction, a plateau, and then a rather abrupt decline in the later years.

As with everything, there is a beginning, and my physical or athletic beginning started seventy years ago when I was eight years old; during the Second World War I was being treated by our family doctor for obesity. The affectionate nickname for me among my New York City street friends was, "Fatboy." It was like being called Jim, only a little different. This condition (the obesity not the nickname) was most likely caused by my eating life-raft emergency rations brought home by my father from the ship building yards in New Jersey, where he helped prepare American Merchant Marine prey for predatory German U-Boats. At three thousand calories per Chunky-sized candy bar , I was eating about ten thousand extra calories a day for quite a while, turning my five foot-four inch body into a roly-poly ball. In the nineteen forties no one seemed to connect the two things - a fat body proportional to ingested calories. At least my doctor did not - although I might not have owned up to the chocolate pilfering.

In 1944, when my dad couldn't stand it any longer he left the safety of a draft deferment as a critical war worker and joined the Marine Corps, ignoring the potentially adverse consequences to him and his family. After Dad left, and the emergency rations left with him, my obesity condition abated somewhat. Can you imagine the shame of a warrior man like my father, propelled by his own demons, who wanted to kill the enemy, who wrestled on black and white television when the screens were five inches in diameter, who boxed in the Marine Corps until age 39, living in this situation? Here was this warrior with a son who resembled the Michelin tire boy; someone you could bury your finger in until it disappeared. It must have been extraordinarily tough on dad's ego; being the father of a lump of lard. Of course, the fallout for me was no picnic.

Between eight and eleven years of age, there was a general thinning out (of me, not the herd, although the war took care of a lot of that in the ranks of the eighteen to twenty two year olds). My weight did not keep me from being athletic, nor do I remember being chosen last for our street teams. Stickball, stoup ball, boxing with sixteen ounce gloves, roller skate hockey, kick the can, billiards, and bicycle rides, were all part of the package. Gang fights didn't come until later.

When I was eleven (in 1947), our family moved to North Carolina, to be near the Marine Corps base. I went to a local - yokel school in Jacksonville, a town three blocks long. It had a Trailways bus station at one end and a Western Electric hardware store at the other, and two movie theaters in between that served fresh, hot popcorn and once in a while you could have your picture taken with a visiting, career is plummeting Hollywood star like Lash LaRue.

Having come from a New York City parochial school, in the two years I was in North Carolina, I did not learn anything new in school unless it was in a subject that I had not had before. Naturally, because of my Yankee accent, I had to fight my way into acceptance, but it did happen. Thank God for my New York fight club. Due to the non-rigorous academic standards, another student and I used to slip off campus to the local pool hall and shoot pool for part of the day. The song "Mule Train," is forever lodged in my memory bank.

Although school was not very beneficial, my time in North Carolina (age 11 to 13) was very educational in many ways. In no particular order of importance I saw students coming to school barefoot; I met a florid-faced, well-to-do, pot-bellied father who liked to parade around the house naked in front of his kids and me; I worked in carnivals picking up the cats people knocked off the shelves with a softball sized ball, and saw things I shouldn't have seen at that age at the Hootchie - Koochie show, which was made extra hot for the young Marines; I went hunting alone with a twelve gauge shotgun and shot my first rabbit, which I ate; I was told by a neighbor-girl my age, that her mother said she couldn't play with me because I was too poor; I learned to masturbate with a group of guys in a circle; I learned to fish in a creek for perch with a bamboo pole and bobber, and I watched the colored people around me catching fish the same way, knowing that it might be the only protein they would get that day; I learned that the ocean is an extraordinarily beautiful place; I learned that when you are poor as a child you usually don't know it; I found that I was good at kicking a football field-goal style, an important athletic activity; I learned walking a mile to school can be fun, especially when part of that walk was over a trestle - especially when the only thing between you and the water below was the railroad ties, and there was no place to hide if a train came along; I learned that really poor people had to teach their children to lie about what they ate for breakfast that day to keep the authorities from taking the children away; I learned that I was frightened of snakes when they appear suddenly out of holes in the ground; I learned to face a lot of fears when in the woods alone; I learned to have fun when in the woods alone; I learned that my pool shooting partner liked his dog to perform fellatio on him in the woods; I learned an entire thesaurus of names for African American people, including, but not limited to, nigger, nigra, negro, colored,

coon, jungle bunny, boy, black-boy and many more, and I learned of
the deep, abiding hate behind the words. Similarly, in that same
thesaurus, I learned that Yankee, and Dammed-Yankee, and God
Dammed Yankee were all the same word; I joined the Boy Scouts
and had a lot of fun, and saved $18 for my first Scout uniform by
earning fifty-cents a day cleaning up the trash around the drive-in
restaurant across the road after school; I got slapped in the face
really hard by my eighth grade teacher, in fact she bounced my head
off the wall; I learned that when the Marines are finished with
maneuvers on an island in the Neuse river, they leave a mess behind,
including edible C-rations, and live bullets in four feet of water that
can be dug out and the gun powder gotten out of them; I learned
that parents, especially fathers, are not always kind and loving; I
learned to be embarrassed, with my sister, when driving through
town in the back of a panel truck, with my drunken father turning
the heads of both blacks and whites towards our truck by singing,
"Good Night Irene" at the top of his lungs; I learned how to work on
a Laundry / Dry Cleaning truck delivering clothes and uniforms
daily to the Marines stationed at Camp LeJeune; I sold newspapers
on the Marine base, and often ate dinner when the Marines were
finished eating - and they really ate good food (veal chops never
crossed our table at home); I learned that the biggest, scariest
looking Marines were the most gentle with me and the other
newspaper kids - they probably had no violence left in them; I
learned to have a smart, pet piglet for one summer while I visited an
aunt and uncle in South Carolina, only to have to mourn the pig
when he died from snakebite at the end of the summer; I learned
how to pick cotton; I learned how a cotton gin works, from
beginning to end, to turn out five-hundred pound bales wrapped in
burlap as the last step; I learned how a ten year old distant cousin
drove a jeep on a red clay road, standing up and going at least fifty
miles an hour, I learned how to slaughter a very large pig and eat
sausage a half hour old. I learned that my uncle's cousin kept a black
man as a hand around the farm, and that man slept on straw in the

barn and was essentially still a slave. God, I learned a lot in those two years, way more than I've listed, but I didn't know I was learning at the time. To me it was just observing life and there was no conscious thought of evaluating this or that. And at the same time I was growing taller and thinner and stronger.

In 1949, we moved back to New York. I went to PS 30 for the last half of the eighth grade, and began to grow taller and thinner. Somewhere in there I had surgery to repair a hernia, and after that I just seemed to spurt upwards (God, what a word choice - here I am a teenager spurting upwards). I only have impressions that I was morphing into a Greek God - well not exactly, but all kids dream, don't they. It offsets the nightmares of reality. As luck would have it, I had developed a southern accent over my two-year immersion in Dixie, and guess what? I had to fight my way back into acceptance in New York, but not as badly because I was mostly among friends.

One of the first things I did on returning to New York was to get a job in the grocery store around the corner so I could buy a pair of roller skates to play roller skate hockey with my friends. Two Jewish brothers owned the store and they were so nice. They hired me to deliver orders on Saturdays. I earned ten-cents per order, and I could keep my tips. I delivered orders, included lugging things like a case of 12 quarts of bottled beer up to the fifth floor in one of the tenement buildings on our street. In between deliveries I had to go with one of the brothers (the big one) to the basement storage room and help him rearrange mounds of stock. Many of the boxes we moved were forty-eight, one-pound cans of this or that. It was pretty taxing, but I think I liked it because I was building my body into something strong. On my first day I earned about seven dollars and that was enough to buy a pair of Chicago, roller skates. They were top of the line and had steel wheels with ball bearings, and metal clamps to clamp them onto your shoes. They were great.

Unfortunately, within a year or two a new thing called a Super Market went in a block away and the grocery store had to close its doors.

Desert Impressions

by Jim Oggerino

Twenty-six floors above the desert.
Isolated, insulated, a microscopic observer.
Night transitions to dawn.
Stark hills silhouette the horizon.
A line of headlights call attention
to the trucks sliding east
hauling California "bread"
to everywhere else.

Driving across the desert floor,
a whispering metal pod
moving Barbara and me
closer to the craggy, barren, peaks,
a special beauty -
if the observer chooses to see it.
The terrain not unlike life from time to time
BITCHIN.

Cresting a hill,
a shock in color, size and texture.
Pyramid Lake,
named after a rock in the middle.
Thoughts drifting a century
to settlers who strained and died
pushing and pulling wagons
over the impersonal terrain
until one day,
the light blue shock.
IMPACT.

Walking on the desert floor.
Sun hardened, cracked, covered with
fine dust that swirls in silent protest
as shoes disturb the domain
that has for so long remained untouched.
Fingers feeling tumbleweed and scrub brush.
Taking pictures of each other,
a freeze frame of desolation
in the midst of abundant life.
Not unlike us from time to time.

Down the road,
a federal wild horse and burro preserve,
a noble effort to save animals from civilization by
rounding them up and selling them to the civilized.
Who knows the tax cost of carting creatures by
helicopter and truck to vet tended pens with
abundant food until adoption or euthanasia.

How 'bout the street children?
Where are the noble and civilized for them?
Can't throw a saddle on kids for fun or work.
Everyone knows the abused are a pain in the ass to
break.
Leave them on the streets
to experience their own
Desert Impressions.

THE WALL

by Jim Oggerino

THREE BRONZE BANDOLIERED WARRIORS
STARE IN AWE, WITH SIGHTLESS EYES,
AT THE EBONY WALL ANNOUNCING
THE VIOLENT, ABRUPT CESSATION OF LIFE
OF FIFTY-EIGHT THOUSAND OF THEIR COMRADES,
FIFTY-EIGHT THOUSAND, THREE HUNDRED AND
SEVENTY-TWO.

TWIN TRIANGLES, ONE POINTING EAST,
THE OTHER WEST,
A SCANT HUNDRED-FIFTY YARDS LONG,
ABOUT SEVENTY-FIVE WHOLE PEOPLE LAID END TO
END, CONTAIN THEIR NAMES IN
TINY ETCHED GRAVES,
TEN INCHES LONG, ONE INCH HIGH AND ONE-EIGHTH
INCH DEEP.
FIFTY-EIGHT THOUSAND, THREE HUNDRED AND
SEVENTY-TWO.

WIDOWS, CHILDREN, PARENTS, SIBLINGS, OLD
FRIENDS, EX-FIANCES, AND THE CURIOUS FILE BY.
THE CHILDREN ARE NOISY-
NOT YET TOUCHED BY DEATH.
SOME VISITORS REACH OUT, TENDERLY
TOUCH A NAME.
OTHERS STENCIL A NAME ON A PIECE OF PAPER-

ALL THEY CAN TAKE HOME
FROM THE LIST OF
FIFTY-EIGHT THOUSAND, THREE HUNDRED AND
SEVENTY-TWO.

CUT BELOW GROUND LEVEL LIKE AN OPEN GRAVE
THE WALL IS CURIOUSLY DEVOID
OF LIVING SOUNDS--
CARS, BUSES, HORNS, LAUGHTER.
ONLY THE ROAR OF JETS FLYING TO THE NEARBY
AIRPORT INTRUDES, IRONICALLY THE LAST SOUND
HEARD BY MANY OF THE
FIFTY-EIGHT THOUSAND, THREE HUNDRED AND
SEVENTY-TWO.

THROUGH COLD GRAY DAYS WITH SLEET,
AND SUNNY DAYS WITH BLUE SKY AND
BILLOWING CLOUDS,
THE WALL REMAINS UNCHANGED,
EXCEPTING THE NEW
FLOWERS, AMERICAN FLAGS AND PHOTOGRAPHS,
PLACED TO MARK THE LAST REMEMBRANCE OF THE
FIFTY-EIGHT THOUSAND, THREE HUNDRED AND
SEVENTY-TWO.

Optimism

by Jim Oggerino

Both the drapes and sliding door
were cracked open four inches – no more.
The outside sun came floating by
and warmed his face. It made him cry
to feel that softly soothing heat,
and he too ill to gain his feet.
The sun slid past that slender crack,
he cried out, "No, no, come back."
He rolled and fell upon the floor,
crawled until he reached the door.
He forced the slider open wider,
felt the warmth and healing power
of the sun upon his neck.
He lay his head upon the deck,
and knew that soon he was to die,
in a cold grave he was to lie.
But he thought with misplaced glee,
"At least you'll grow grass over me!"

Dogs and Planetary Motion

by Jim Oggerino

I have a cute little dog. He is an all-black pug, so we named him Black Jack. He is 27 pounds of fun, but is often a pain in the neck too. Gratefully, at a year and three quarters old, he is settling down some.

During these late summer months, the early morning sun shines through our dining room slider leaving a sun spot wherever it hits the floor. Because he is so tired from waking up and eating, Jack likes to take a post breakfast nap and do some sun worshiping. He lies in the sunspots that appear on the dining room chairs or carpet with his face pointed towards the sunshine. He usually starts in one of the chairs and as the sun moves on he goes to the floor and follows along as needed to keep up with the motion of the sun, until his little no-nose is pressed against the slider glass.

As with many dogs, when Jack can't get something because it is out his reach he will scratch for it with his front paws. For example, when we are playing fetch with a tennis ball or a stuffed toy and it goes under a piece of furniture, he scratches like crazy to get at the ball or toy. With his sharp little claws, this is not good for the furniture, especially for leather furniture, so I get up and get him what he is trying to get and we continue the game. He stops scratching and we have some more fun.

However, a few days ago I was unable to help Jack. He was on his favorite dining room chair basking in the sun. All of a sudden I heard this ferocious scratching and checked to see what was going on. It seems that the sun had traversed the sky such that there was only a three-inch by three-inch patch left on one corner of the chair's seat cushion. I could tell that Jack was trying to move the sunspot back to the middle of the chair so he could enjoy it a little longer. I knew then that dogs do not make good astrophysicists.

Norma Slavit

I first heard about Louise Webb's Memoirs Class from a friend who was a member of the National League of American Pen Women. I had attended a Memoirs Class in Cupertino, but this class was closer for me to attend. I found Louise led a very informative class and I appreciate her approach.

I was born and lived in San Francisco until I married. I'm a graduate of San Francisco State University and did my graduate work at Hunter College in New York as well as the University of San Francisco. I am a former master teacher who taught in the elementary schools of New Rochelle, New York, and San Francisco. I also taught music at Hillbrook, a private school in Los Gatos.

For over ten years I was a newspaper editor for the Jewish Community Center (JCC) in Palo Alto. My position included being the marketing and public relations manager. Many of my articles and stories have appeared in educational journals, magazines, and newspapers. I have one published play to my credit, and an early story appeared in the Encyclopedia Britannica reading series.

A highlight of my career was when I had the pleasure of interviewing the honorable, Norm Mineta, when he was mayor, for a feature article in the San Jose Mercury News.

Along with the Mercury's cameraman, I shadowed the mayor as he went about his typical day in Japan Town. We strolled the streets, stopping to visit merchants along the way. Later, he allowed me to interview him for a book I was working on (but never published) which dealt with his life in the internment camp when he was a child during the war years.

My husband passed away 13 years ago. We have two children and three grandchildren. I am engaged to, Paul, a wonderful man who I met on Valentine's Day seven years ago.

I am a member of the Society of Children's Book Writers and Illustrators as well as the National League of American Pen Women.

I have published two children's books, *Peaches, Frog and the Man in the Moon* for the four to eight year old child, and *September Thanksgiving,* a chapter book for the nine to thirteen year old student. Both are available on Amazon.com.

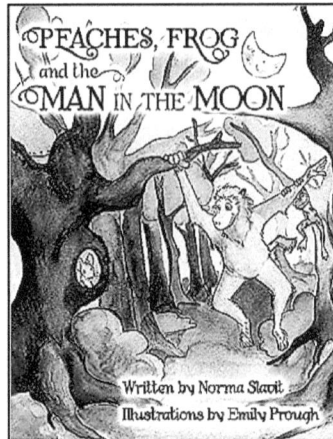

Summer Vacation at Grandma Hannah's House

by Norma Slavit

They say life is not so much about the destination as the journey. The result of one summer journey to Oroville, California, when I was about eight or nine, left a mark on my memory that still remains with me today.

The year was around 1940. The weather was typical for a San Francisco summer. It was the time in our air-conditioned city when the dependable fog and cool ocean breezes left many with a yearning to find a place in the sun. Our place in the sun was Grandma's country house in Oroville, California. Joyce Biancalana and her mother accepted the invitation to join us. We packed our bags and headed for the warmth of Oroville and Grandma Hannah's country house in the Sacramento Valley.

Grandma Hannah lived alone in a house that was surrounded by an acre of fruit and nut trees. Grandma was on a first name basis with all her rabbits, chickens and other farm animals. Before I could bring myself to eat one of Grandma's delicious meals, I had to be thoroughly convinced that one of her farm animals somehow didn't end up on my plate.

Going inside Grandma's house was like entering a time machine – traveling back, back to another time and place. I was eager to point out everything to Joyce, like the mysterious wires that dangled from the ceiling and continued on a narrow path along the staircase to the second floor. (How these wires caused a disastrous fire will be described in another chapter) Joyce was more impressed

219

by the living room furniture, especially the large tapestry that covered one entire wall. It had a pastoral scene of girls in old fashioned clothes who were jumping through hoops.

The first thing I investigated was Grandma's old Victrola machine located in one corner of the room. Like a docent in a museum, I began to demonstrate how I could operate this miraculous machine. First I had to wind its protruding handle round and around, 100 times. A tiny needle was attached to the end of a big arm on top of the machine. Below the arm a record was spinning and spinning, just waiting for someone like me to discover its hidden treasure.

"Bet you have never seen one of these machines," I said to Joyce.

Suddenly, the big arm dropped from my grasp. Down came the Victrola's arm landing right in the middle of a record. Strange, scratchy, moaning, whaling sounds suddenly blasted out from this wonderful music machine, sending Grandma hurrying into the room.

"Let's be a good girl and not play around with Grandma's Victrola," she exclaimed as she shooed me away from the mysterious wooden treasure.

Not discouraged, I made a beeline to the other music machine in the living room – an old upright piano. Before demonstrating this magnificent machine, I took a flying ride on the piano stool.

"Watch me, Joyce," I called out to my best friend. "You can have a turn next."

One large translucent glass marble was attached to the bottom of each of the stool's legs. The antique stool rested majestically on the colorful living room carpet. As I pushed myself round and round, the stool made a funny creaking sound. Higher and higher I went. Joyce waited patiently for her turn as I pushed the tired old stool to its limits and was finally sent crashing to the ground. Once again, Grandma came into the room. This, however, didn't stop me from exploring and performing on the old piano's wonderful chipped white keys. I could have played for hours, if it wasn't for our mothers who sent Joyce and me outdoors to play and followed us there.

Outdoors, there were more treasures for two city girls to explore. Oblivious to the oppressive heat, I was in the middle of introducing Joyce to Grandma's animals, when our mothers decided it was too hot to stay on the farm. We were whisked away for a short walk to the levee so we could go wading in what was called "the ole swimming hole." It was a short walk from Grandma's farm.

The scenic, peaceful landscape was a photographer's dream. On one side of the road, endless orange groves followed the meandering Feather River just as far as the eye could see. It was the first time Joyce had seen an orange growing from a tree. They were the largest oranges I had ever seen and they seemed to create an apron of orange dots that skirted the river's edge. Squinting through blurred vision, I imagined seeing thousands of trees with big orange balls hanging from them like Christmas tree lights.

Upstream, we could see a gigantic machine stuck in the water. I was told it was an old dredger, a relic from gold miner's days. We would learn later that gold had been discovered long ago, in this area.

When we arrived at the swimming hole our mother's sat down on wooden bleachers. They gave us strict safety rules since this was not a city swimming pool and there were no life guards.

The first thing Joyce and I noticed were boys climbing the huge, tall trees that shaded the area. We watched in awe as they climbed to the top of the trees.

"Don't you wish we could join them?" Joyce asked.

"Not a chance with our mom's watching," I answered.

The two boys provided us with a wonderful show. When they had climbed to the top of the trees, they reached out to grab long, thick ropes that were attached to the tree limbs. It was like a jungle scene from a movie. What great entertainment! We watched them swing from the tree, back and forth just like Tarzan. Suddenly, we gasped in delight. The boys dropped like arrows straight down into the Feather River, disappeared from sight, then came up to the water's surface greeted by clapping and cheering from on lookers.

Joyce and I looked at them wistfully wishing we too could climb those trees and dive into the water. Since neither of us could even swim, and our mother's watchful eyes were on us at all times, we were content to just wade at the water's edge. In front of us was a little dock floating in the middle of the river. It was skirted by the ropes on each side so that swimmers, who dared, could swim out to the dock and sun themselves. These chosen few, the lucky ones who could swim out to the dock, looked back at us in a boastful way that seemed to dare Joyce and me to join them. But of course, we were stranded at the edge of the shore. Close by, seated on the bleachers, my mother and Joyce's mother, Bruno, relaxed under the sun's penetrating rays protected by their sun parasols. They kept a watchful eye on us I as we waded in the crystal clear water.

It was fun to collect the colorful rocks our toes caught as we walked. I loved the feel of the cool water as it splashed up the sides of my legs tickling them. The smooth rocks provided a firm foot massage as I pressed my feet down into them.

We were at a blissful age when we didn't have a care in the world. We were not yet bothered by the opinion of others or by the body changes that would soon consume our thoughts and actions in the next few years. Two innocent young girls wading in the clear cool waters on a balmy summer day in the country were far away from fog, city traffic and any worries. That is until the unthinkable happened.

Suddenly, the rocky ground under me gave way and I dropped off into never-never land, disappearing into the water. Seeing her only child disappear from sight, Mother jumped up from the bleachers. Still carrying that sun parasol, she ran to the water crying out, "Please someone help me. My daughter is drowning! She's drowning."

It seemed like an eternity until I finally bobbed up to the surface. How, I hated the feeling of water swishing in my eyes and ears. I coughed out part of the river I had swallowed. My head was throbbing from the fright of losing my foothold and sinking into the unknown abyss. Most of all, I think what scared me enough to leave a lasting impression, was the dreaded look of shock on my mother's face and upon hearing those words for the first time, "she's drowning."

They say life is about the journey. I took something with me from that summer trip to Oroville which still plaques me today. In spite of the fact that several people have tried in vain to teach me how to swim, I have never been able to relax enough to let go of that fear of drowning.

The Fourth Pedal

by Norma Slavit

After the Great Depression, well into the 1940's, the years were financially challenging for my parents. Mother had to keep a strict written budget and record all her expenses in a special notebook book. Music was our only luxury.

Once each month dad brought home a classical music album or special record which he purchased at Sherman & Clay, our favorite music store in San Francisco. If I was lucky, dad would take me along for a trip downtown to the music store. It was always a special adventure for me. The excitement began when we entered a sound proof room where dad could play a myriad of recordings until he found the right musician playing with the symphony orchestra of dad's choice. If dad wanted a recording of Chopin, than the pianist had to be Brailovsky, who was known for performing the best interpretation of Chopin's music. If we selected a German composer, the artist had to be Arthur Snabel, and so it went. At the end of our visit, when we made our purchase, dad had to be completely satisfied. After all, we were on a strict budget, and only the best would do. Mom could hardly wait for the moment when we arrived home so we could all sit down and enjoy hearing the treasured record of the month.

Mom's favorite composer was Strauss and Franz Liszt. Dad preferred Beethoven and Chopin. Rachmaninoff was my favorite. Before I was born, Mom had sung with a choral group led by Madam Vough. This group had the honor of being selected to sing at the San Francisco World's Fair. Since there was always music around me, it was no wonder that I developed a love for classical music at a young age.

"If only we could have a piano," I told my parents over and over again. Of course, a piano was out of the question, something **we could not afford**.

My parents thought their money problems would ease up if only dad could find a job that paid more than his position with Sommer & Kaufmann's fine shoe company. After some time had passed he left his job to become a substitute mail carrier. One day his fellow mail carriers presented dad with a special challenge. They told him the next exam for positions as permanent postal employees was being held soon and they dared my dad to try to pass the test. Everyone, except dad, knew the exam was quite difficult and required intense study. None of his buddies had passed the test yet. In those days, the test included a knowledge of advanced math, the San Francisco train and boat schedules and an emphasis on memorization. The postal employees knew that dad, who still had a little German accent, had only recently received his citizenship papers. No one thought he could pass the difficult exam so they dared him to take it. Since my father could never pass up a dare, he studied and took the exam.

We were thrilled when Dad came home from his route one day and announced he had passed the postal exam with flying colors. Now, he would have the security of being a permanent government employee. Perhaps with the small increase in salary Mother wouldn't have to continue making so many sacrifices-- doing without nylon hose or a new dress. At her insistence, she urged dad to save as much money as possible in order to make a down payment on a new home. Dad reminded Mother that if we were going to leave apartment living behind, it probably meant we wouldn't be able to afford the new records we looked forward to each month, and mother's many sacrifices would have to continue.

A construction company, Hansen Brothers, was building new homes in the upper Engleside district of South San Francisco. The location was excellent for schools and transportation. In one direction, the K street car ran along Ocean Avenue (two blocks away) and, in the other direction, one block away, the 26 Daly City bus traveled along San Jose Avenue. We did not have a car, but the city had such good transportation, we didn't seem to need one. The new neighborhood had everything--Balboa Park, schools, a junior museum for me; and excellent transportation for dad. The only thing lacking was good grocery stores nearby. At the time, I had just finished third grade at Thomas Edison Elementary School. Mom selected an area where she believed we could live forever.

We watched our "dream home" being built from the ground up. It turned out to be our first and only home. Mom had done her research well. All the schools were within walking distance for me. San Miguel Grammar School was four to five blocks away, James Denman Junior High was across the street from San Miguel and Balboa High was just across the street from the Junior High. Even San Francisco City College was a short eight blocks away.

What fun it was taking the street car out to the new site to watch the progress of homes being built on Niagara Avenue. The new development was on flat land, very close to the hills. Three blocks away, I remember seeing the remnants of sand dunes which were slowly being removed to make room for new homes. Our new address was 530 Niagara Avenue.

The home, which seemed magnificent to me, was in the middle of the block. It had two bedrooms and one large bathroom. The living room faced the street as did the dining room. A small kitchen was attached to the dining room. The kitchen area had a huge skylight in the middle of the room. Brick stairs led up to the front door, and the house had a huge basement the size of the entire house. There was a very small front and back yard. All this for the outrageous sum of $5,000. It would take my father some 30 years to pay off the mortgage.

The homes were called "attached homes," because there was a home on either side with no space in between. Joyce Biancalana, a girl who was one year younger than I, lived with her family next door. A childless couple, Joe and Dell Merten, lived on the other side. We affectionately called Joe Mr. Encyclopedia, because he was so knowledgeable about any subject.

In short time, we settled into our new home. Dad had to get up much earlier now since we were further away from the main post office where he worked. Before the sun rose each morning while I was sleeping, mom was in the kitchen by four o'clock preparing dad's usual breakfast: grapefruit, two soft boiled eggs, toast and coffee sweetened by a spoonful of honey. She felt it was her duty or "role" to get dad off to a good start each day so he could face the exhausting life a mailman encountered. It was exhausting, not only because of the early hour, but dad's route was climbing one of the steepest hills in San Francisco – Telegraph Hill. Today, the law states that a postal carrier can carry no more than 70 pounds on his back. In those days, there was no weight limit.

Dad's route began in the North Beach area of the city. With parcels and mail weighing in at 100 pounds or more tucked into a heavy leather mail bag slung over his shoulder, dad began ascending the steep hills of San Francisco. He went all the way to the top of the highest hill which dead-ended at the magnificent Coit Tower. Dad climbed that route in rain, sleet, hot or cold weather, up and down the hills. It's a good thing he loved the outdoors and was a dedicated carrier who enjoyed his job.

Dad delivered mail to some of the San Francisco's most prominent residents which included Lefty O'Doul (of Giants baseball fame) and Mr. Ghiradelli of chocolate fame. He was the only carrier who made sure his customers received their mail early around seven or eight o'clock each morning. Often, dad went out to make two deliveries. It was no wonder his customers respected and loved him. He would go out of his way to please. If he knew someone was expecting a special package, he made an extra trip to get it for them. News of one letter in dad's mail sack appeared in the San Francisco *Chronicle.* I believe Herb Caen, the famous news columnist, printed it. In place of an address, the following information was scribbled across the front of the envelope: "go up the hill to that winding street, turn left at the street light, then down one more block to the house with green shutters." Any other carrier would have placed this in the "dead letter" file. Not my dad. He actually found the house, and delivered the letter!

Many of dad's patrons met dad at their door and came out to chat with him. They soon learned all about our family, especially my love for music. Maxi, as he was endearingly known to all, became everyone's friend. One lady on his route did a remarkable thing. Since a prominent pianist was in town performing, she invited the gentleman to her home for a private concert. Her guests included selected dignitaries. Imagine our surprise when we learned she also invited her mailman, my dad, to her soirée. She knew that I had a love for classical music, and had invited me to attend also.

On the day in memory, I was 11 or 12 years old. It was the perfect time for dad to show me his route. All the way up those steep hills he stopped to point out interesting views. As Coit Tower got closer and closer in sight, dad stopped and proudly pointed to the homes of his prominent customers, many of whom were celebrities.

I was dazzled by the breathtaking view as we entered the home where the private concert was being held. I believe there was a view of the Golden Gate Bridge from the huge windows that draped the immense living room. Chairs had been placed in a semi-circle around the most beautiful baby grand piano I had ever seen. There was a chair for dad in the front row. An over-sized velvet cushion had been placed for me on the floor, right next to the piano legs. From this vantage point, I could watch the pianist's fingers fly up and down the keys as he played spiraling arpeggios and glissandos. I remember feeling uneasy sitting there for all to see, so close to the piano. However, as soon as the pianist began playing, my embarrassment faded away as I was transported to some magical place where I was free to dream wondrous pictures the music put in my head.

The most remarkable thing happened after the concert. A customer took dad aside and said, "I notice how involved your daughter is with the music, Maxi. Now that I am moving, I can only take one of my pianos with me. How would you like to have my upright for your daughter?" she asked.

I had to pinch myself to find out if I was dreaming. My father, however, reassured me that we were going to get a piano at last! I don't know who paid to have the piano delivered, but it took four men to get the heavy old piano into our living room. I can't remember if it came through the front door or by way of the living room window. What I do remember, is that my life changed dramatically with the arrival of that piano.

Mother was quick to polish the piano's dark mahogany wood to a mirror bright glow. I checked out the ivory keys, and dad sat back and watched his family marvel around the most treasured object in

the entire house. A stool came with the piano. It had glass marbles at the bottom on the legs and the mahogany piano stool squeaked when turned.

This piano was a unique piano for it had something rarely seen in any other piano. **It had a fourth pedal.** When I pressed my foot down on the fourth pedal, we were all amazed at the results. Each time I played a key, and simultaneously pressed down on the fourth pedal, we heard what sounded like a banjo and violin accompaniment. It sounded like a player piano. For a long time it was a conversation piece and a source of great amusement for those who had the patience to listen.

We couldn't afford a piano teacher, so mother became my first teacher. She was excellent but one day she said to dad, "Norma is progressing very fast. I have taken her as far as I can. With her talent, she is ready for a professional piano teacher." One day when Dad's mother, Grandma Martha, came for a visit, she learned of my need for a teacher.

"Who are you to afford piano lessons for Norma on a mailman's salary?" she said trying to convince us with her heavy German accent, "Piano lessons are for rich people."

Thank goodness mom stood her ground once again and the search for a piano teacher began. We didn't have to look far, because one of my girlfriends told us about her teacher. Mrs. Steffans lived out in the avenues quite a distance away, and my girlfriend asked if I could go with her to meet the teacher.

Mother looked over her budget and cut out all the things she felt she could do without. The new curtains would have to wait. She would find a way to pay for my piano lessons. I don't know how they managed it but in the end, I became Mrs. Steffan's new piano student.

I will always be grateful for my parent's decision. Eventually, I became a piano teacher, played in many recitals and concerts, and taught music in the public and private schools.

What happened to that wonderful old piano? Where is the unique piano that boasts of a fourth pedal? Today, that family piano sits in my daughter's living room. My grandchildren Rachel and Joshua show a profound interest in music and I have started giving them what I call "music readiness lessons."

As to the question of the piano's background, there are two possibilities: 1) The piano was once in a famous San Francisco theatre where silent movies were shown to the background accompaniment of the fourth pedal. 2) That famous grand old upright was once in a saloon where the 49'ers, of Gold Rush days would place their drinks on the piano top

We will never know for sure, which of the two theories is the correct one. What I do know for certain is that the piano will forever be out of tune and that the fourth pedal stopped working years ago. One can only imagine the poignant turn-of-the-century stories that are hidden deep beneath the layers of built up wax my mother once lovingly applied over the upright's satin smooth rich wood veneer.

When my parents passed away, neither of my two children said they had room for the family piano. Finally after a lot of persuasion, my daughter agreed to have it in her back bedroom. When the movers arrived they could not get the tall upright, bulky heavy piano around the corners of her house, so it had the stately position of being placed in the living room.

After a while, my daughter seemed to take pride polishing the rich, dark mahogany veneer in much the same way as my mother once did. The top of the piano became a center piece for family photos just as it once was in my mother's house. As to the fourth pedal, the stories remain hidden behind a pedal that once was connected to something that produced a rinky-dink accompaniment. That pedal is still silenced and no one knows the hidden stories of its role in early San Francisco, unless I have told them. As to the function of the piano today, I gave each of my grandchildren music lessons on a piano that is rich on history but poor on quality of tone.

Somehow, I think my parents would be grateful if they knew the amazing San Francisco piano that a wealthy celebrity once gave to her mailman, still remains in our family, bringing joy to those who would stop, spend a while, and pause to caress its faded ivory keys.

231

Teacher or Policewoman?

by Norma Slavit

Dedicated to the memory of my dear friend, Gladys Robinson

Popee perched himself precariously on the window's inside ledge of the two-story brick school building. Threatening to jump, he straddled his legs across the window sill, shifting from one leg to the other as he glanced over his shoulder to see how many of his second grade class mates were watching him. He knew he had the teacher's attention!

The place was Bay View Elementary School located in San Francisco's notorious Hunter's Point district. The year was 1954. It was a year when over 400 qualified teachers applied for a position in the city. I was one of the fortunate few who made the list. Having just graduated from San Francisco State College, this was my first assignment. In fact, it was my first week!

"I'm gon'na jump," Popee announced. "What you gon'na do, teacher?"

What could I do? Nothing could have prepared me for this moment. There wasn't a college or a text in existence that gave advice for this scenario. I knew I had only a micro-moment to decide.

If I attempted a rescue and bolted to his side making an effort to remove Popee from the ledge, he could impress the class and easily jump out the window before I got to his side. On the other hand, if I tried to reason with him, he might still jump. Quickly, I mouthed a silent prayer to the dear Lord, seeking guidance.

Cutting into the chilled silence, from the back of the room Popee's classmate, Hector, reveled in the moment of panic and yelled out to me, "We got rid of our last teacher – we'll get rid of you too."

Collectively, the class looked first at Popee and then at me. The seconds ticked away. The only audible noise came from the loud, fast pounding of my heart.

At that moment, Popee made his move. He jumped!

He jumped right back into the room, tucked himself into a ball and rolled up and down the aisles of the second grade classroom.

I made my move also. I attempted to ignore the disturbed second grader and tried to bring the class' attention back to the lesson at hand. Thank goodness the strategy worked. When the boys and girls saw that I ignored Popee, they also tried to ignore him.

Class focus returned to the lesson and the teacher. Popee lost that round, but if his tactics hadn't worked on this day, rest assured, he would try another way to get attention in the near future. The next time, I would be ready for him.

This second grade class was a compilation of many emotionally disturbed children including those with multiple problems. There were no suitable Special Ed classes in those days. The principal decided not to give this assignment to a tenured teacher. No, it would serve as a "testing ground" for the new teacher. Me. The sad fact was that some wonderful students who really wanted to learn were thrown into this strange mix.

I went into teaching because I love children. My goal was to bring enriching learning experiences into the class each day, to awaken my students' senses, help each boy and girl strive to reach his/her potential and to make learning fun, a challenge and a complete joy. These things are only possible when there is order in the room. Popee, Hector and other students in my second grade class presented a difficult discipline problem. They created an environment that, at times, turned me into a policewoman as well as a teacher.

I wanted my students to look forward to each day at school. As for me, the challenge of this class was so great that I began to count the days until the weekend. After my first week of initiation as a new teacher, I had a short conversation with my parents. The explanation for my future behavior went something like this:

"Mom and dad, I am determined to overcome a bad situation and be successful. I am going to succeed as a teacher. However, I will need your help and understanding. Please forgive me, but for the next few months you will see me only briefly for meals. I will spend most of my time locked in the bedroom, correcting class papers, making charts and preparing exciting lesson plans. Take a good look at me now, because by the end of this semester you will see your daughter age five years right before your eyes. Please hang in there with me.

My second grade classroom was right next door to Mrs. Stager, the principal. On a few occasions, she would open my door, take a quick glance around the room then, appearing satisfied, she left without ever entering the room. She must have known I could have used help. No help came. During lunch break, I was usually too busy correcting papers and making plans to join the other teachers. It was a great ethnic group of dedicated teachers and in time, several of them became my good friends. However, Gladys Robinson was the only teacher who came to my rescue.

One day, that first month of teaching, Gladys appeared in my room with a treat. "I think I know why we are not seeing you in the lunch room," she said. "You see, I had Hector and Popee in first grade. Welcome to Bay View." With that, she shook my hand and gave me a box of home-made sweets.

Gladys became my mentor and good friend. She and her husband Jimmy lived on Caine Street, about five minutes from my parent's home. They invited me to drive to school with them, until I had saved up money to purchase my first car. At her suggestion, Gladys spent many hours with me after school in her home showing me how to make a myriad of class charts. She had a wealth of suggestions. I survived that first semester with her help. I never forgot Gladys or her kindness. Not only was she a sterling example of an excellent teacher, but she was a wonderful person. I was invited to many special occasions at her home and soon got to know her entire family. We shared many experiences together.

Three years later when Herb and I got married, I was proud to invite Gladys and Jimmy to our wedding. They were the only African-Americans in a sea of Caucasian faces.

1956 was a time when race divided many people in our country. Prejudice was hidden well, but existed nevertheless. No color barrier existed between my friend Gladys and me. In a way, you might say we were "color blind." We shared many wonderful memories and I was invited to the Robinson family outings frequently. Gladys and her husband Jim were sterling examples of a happy married couple. The respect, kindness and love they showed for one another impressed me.

Gladys taught me many lessons. Some had to do with teaching. The rest had to do with life. *

* Gladys' husband Jim worked in San Francisco also. Jim Robinson was the first African-American principal of an elementary school located in a major city.

Her brother was the first African-American to work in a major university. He taught at UC, Berkeley.

Sculpture, Sculptor

by Norma Slavit

Written on the fourth year of Herb's passing, 2007. Inspired by a lecture on "coping with loss".

A whimsical rhyme written when I was very young by my father, Max Kaufmann:

> *"Norma Fay*
> *Ran away*
> *She'll come back*
> *Some other day."*

The shell was once solid
then hollow . . .
and now
a work in progress

In the beginning
the sculpture was molded
into the desired shape

Child, student

Over time
a new form emerged

Adult

Again the sculpture changed

The dutiful and appreciative daughter
teacher, employee, writer, musician

devoted and loving bride.
Slowly, pieces were drawn from the shape's core.
And the sculpture took on a new form:

Loyal, dedicated wife
volunteer, daughter-in-law

The metamorphosis continued
bit by bit more pieces
were chiseled from the core

The sculptor, never completely satisfied with the sculpture,
constantly changed the creation.

Its shape and form remolded
with each new role

Mother, friend, teacher,
mother-in-law
grandmother.

Caregiver, caregiver,
caregiver again.

Erosion

Like the side of a mountain,
changed by the elements,
so, too, did the form of the sculpture wear away.

Then silence.

One day work on the sculpture came to an abrupt stop!

Silence

W I D O W   WIDOW!

Bit by bit, so much had been extracted from the
sculpture's form that its core became hollow.
The empty shell weakened and then
was threatened by possible collapse.

Widow. Widow. Widow.
Silence

Over time, the sculptor began to try and fill the hollow shell
new pieces were added where they had once been
chiseled away.

How did the sculptor replace missing pieces?
What strengthened the fragile sculpture?
What new roles helped reshape the sculpture
as well as the sculptor?

Grandmother, Friend, Student, Group Organizer, Writer,
Widow.

When the time was right, the sculptor began to rebuild the
sculpture, piece by piece, bit by bit.

Time. Time to reshape the form and try to fill in the hollow
core that perhaps can never be completely filled again.

Time.

Trying to create a new form

that once again can stand and face the elements

Time.

Love. Love Conflict Love

CANCER cancer   cancer
The struggle
Challenge

Day by day

Power of a number
CA 125
The test
Patient #0396520

The wait

In the beginning
the sculpture was molded
into the desired shape

In the end
the sculpture was rebuilt
not as strong as before
but stronger   A work in progress.

The end became the beginning,
A new rhyme:

"Norma Fay, never ran away.
Listen, please listen.
There are so many things
She still wants to do and say."

Lasting Soles, Loving Souls

by Norma Slavit

"Throw them out. They're too old."

"If you haven't used it in a year, you'll never use it."

These are the expressions friends and family used to try to convince me to give away or throw out some of the things that were taking up space in our closet.

"Mom, look, here's something I gave you five years ago. When is the last time you wore it?" my daughter asked as she dangled a blouse in front of me like a flag, at half-mast.

I was embarrassed, almost to the point of taking action. I wonder if I could use these tactics on my husband to convince him to start weeding out our closet clutter. It was worth a try. I might start with his old pair of shoes which he must have bought over 15 years ago and had not worn in the past five years. It was worth a try. He would never miss them, especially if he hadn't worn them in 15 years!

There is a story behind Herb's shoes that I would like to share. My beloved husband had a difficult time finding comfortable shoes because his foot was long and wide. Therefore, whenever he tired on a well-made pair of shoes that were comfortable, he felt it was important to purchase two pairs, even though they might be the same color and style. With that in mind, over the years, he had collected quite a few pairs of shoes. Often, I asked, even gently threatened to throw out shoes that were worn beyond recognition. However, Herb reminded me, "Norma, good shoes that fit are like old friends. You don't discard them, you keep them!"

240

Besides, he never told me to give away or throw out any of my old things. Winning his point, Herb kept those old brown walking shoes under the bed or tucked away in his closet. Even though they were out of sight, I knew they were still in the house, taking up valuable space.

One day, many months later, I secretly hatched a plan to confiscate those shoes, waiting a long time until I was sure he hadn't worn them and wouldn't miss them. My plot was to put the shoes in the bottom of a bag labeled "for Good Will". On top of the shoes I stuffed a lot of used clothes, then tucked the bag in back of our van. On my next trip to the Good Will store, I would be rid of those shoes forever!

The subject of the shoes never came up again. I even forgot that they were in that Good Will bag in back of the van . . . until one day Herb inquired about the mysterious bag filled with clothes. Feeling clever about the way I had hidden the shoes in the bottom, I pulled out a few of my old clothes from the top of the heap and assured Herb they were just old, unwanted clothes to give away. He never asked again. My plan had worked. I was in the clear.

Fast Forward

Then tragedy hit. One day my beloved husband was diagnosed with colon cancer. We lived life one day at a time, but it was Herb who pulled us up with his courage, determination and hope. Months of chemotherapy went by. Good days and bad days passed. Highs and lows—valleys and peaks. This dreaded disease took its toll. Yet, Herb faced each day with strength, never complaining. At the time, he was still working. Herb was the leading school psychologist for one of the largest California high school districts. He worked with students and faculty all day then drove to his chemo treatments in the late afternoon. Most of his colleagues had no idea he was battling cancer.

On top of everything Herb had to endure, one day he had a terrible, painful attack of gout that hit his big toe with a vengeance.

The toe was so inflamed and swollen that he could not fit into any of his shoes. He had to drive to Kaiser Hospital in summer sandals but even these irritated his toe. Then, like a light bulb going off in his thoughts, Herb suddenly remembered those old brown shoes. He looked all over the house for them. Of course, they were nowhere to be found. Exhausted and weary, Herb turned to me and as a last resort he asked, "Norma you haven't seen those old shoes have you? I knew they might come in handy someday. Please tell me you didn't throw them out."

I sighed and swallowed hard, trying to hide my feelings of dread, which I imagined now was revealed in the worried frown that had frozen my face. I couldn't remember if I had given that Good Will bag away.

"Wait a moment. I'll search the garage," was the weak reply that squirmed out of my mouth. I ran to the car. "Please God let the shoes still be there," I silently prayed.

By this time, there were now several bags piled in the back of my van. They were all earmarked for the Good Will. I panicked. Like a desperate person who is looking for a missing six-carat diamond ring, I ripped open each bag, letting odd pieces of clothes, bric-a-brac and unwanted household items fly about helter-skelter. My hand went to the bottom of each bag searching, searching and feeling for something that felt like coarse leather. I knew I didn't have much more time, Herb would start getting worried and come looking for me.

Then, my prayers were answered. It was like winning the lottery. My hands gripped a pair of shoes. I pulled them out from the bottom, looked at them lovingly and held them to my heart for a moment. As fast as my legs could take me, I ran back into the house with those tattered, worn, ugly ... but prized pair of shoes.

Herb quickly reached out for them; but I held on tightly and would not let Herb put on his own shoes. For the first time, I bent down at his side and tenderly, with great care not to touch his big toe, I put those comfortable old shoes on Herb's swollen foot. They went on like a slipper.

"They don't hurt," he said standing up. "Look," Herb was elated and relieved, perhaps he could tell I was even happier. "Now, I can get to the chemo appointment in time for my treatment. See, honey, you never know when old things might come in handy. And to think of it, Norma, you were the one who wanted to throw them out. Sure glad you didn't!"

And so it came to pass that, like old friends, those shoes, size 13 wide, took my husband to the hospital for his treatment.

It's been twelve years since my beloved Herb passed away and you might wonder if those shoes ever got to the Good Will store. They are not under the bed anymore or in the closet, hidden from view. On the contrary, those shoes can be seen every day outside our front door. Strange, but they don't seem as unsightly as they once appeared to me. They are a welcome sight when I approach my front door. Now, they remind me of sentries watching over our house, the way Herb once watched over me. Those worn, tattered old brown shoes guard our door reminding me of how Herb was once there to protect me.

Although, it's been a long time since I lost my beloved husband, I can't bring myself to throw out those shoes. Perhaps, just perhaps, I will never be able to part with the shoes I was once so eager to cast out.

Cavern of Hidden Thoughts

by Norma Slavit

The coal miner approaches the mine armed with only a pick, an ax and a single light that is attached to the end of his helmet. He gets into the narrow wire cage, and is lowered slowly into an unknown abyss.

Light is squeezed away from him as the miner enters a world of darkness. The air thins as he descends deep into the bowels of the earth. The signal is given to stop and the miner opens the door to explore a vein in the cave. He picks at a spot and chips away at the area, trying to see as much as the light on his helmet will allow.

Carefully, he puts the remnants from his discovery into a leather pouch, enters the cage and gives the signal for those above to bring him up to the surface. He has had it for one day, and is eager to let the light of day reveal the treasure stored away in his pouch. The miner knows he will return to the cave tomorrow, ready to explore more unknown treasure, eager to revisit the site.

I am like that miner chipping away in the cavern of hidden thoughts, hoping to strike a rich vein that will release a flood of memories for me to capture and explore. Capturing memories from my past, digging into an area that has been repressed for so long reminds me of the miner who brings up unexpected treasures. Perhaps it is not treasure to others, but these memoirs which I am attempting to uncover and reveal will give my grandchildren a glimpse of what life was like and what I was like when I was young. In turn, someday, I hope they will pass these memories on to their grandchildren and record their own unique chapter of life for future generations.

Dee Steward

I became a member of the Memoirs Class by accident when my friend, Mabel Brix, called needing a ride to class because her car wouldn't start. I brought her to class at the Saratoga Senior Center and asked, "What time shall I pick you up?" Mabel asked, "Why don't you come on in and see what the class is like?" So I did.

I've been attending Louise Webb's Class for about eight years now and it's been fun. I've met some really nice people! Some are beginners, like I was, and others have been keeping their memoir notes for ages. Some may publish one day and others just wanted to see how much they could remember of their past.

Louise would sometimes suggest topics to write about, just to jog our memories, and I seem to remember some general guidelines like, "Try to avoid politics, religion, gory operations, X-rated experiences and gossip."

When we had written something and read it to the class, we would get a gentle critique from Louise and the class members. All were helpful and positive.

I learned that a memoir doesn't need to be written in chronological order, but to begin by writing down memories as they come to you. Before long, the accumulation of these notes will develop into a "timeline." I have surprised myself by developing my memory in more detail than I would have imagined I could. The memoirs class has helped me "hone" my writing skills.

Who will read my memoirs one day? Who Knows?

I do know that I would be thrilled to read anything written by my mom or grandmothers about their experiences, good, bad, or funny, or anything about their hopes and dreams.

Maybe my memoir will be like a "message in a bottle," found by a descendant yet unborn.

An Excerpt from 1963 in Belgium
The Assassination of President Kennedy

by Dee Steward

Our young family had been in Belgium for months and no one had ever made eye contact or spoken to me. We lived in an apartment in the Embassy district in Brussels. Every day I bundled the baby into her pram and set out on my marketing rounds—a different shop for each type of food—and I was slowly picking up a 'Market list' of French vocabulary—but aside from, "oui, non, merci," that was about all I could say.

We had no television or radio, and rarely saw an English newspaper. I was loving the experience, though, and I soon adapted myself into the 'no-nonsense, deadpan expression' of the people I saw on the street. It was just that I felt invisible.

One freezing November day as I was pushing the pram to the little corner market, a distinguished looking, well dressed gentleman, came walking toward me speaking urgently about something in rapid French!

Startled, my reflex was to smile!

But as he continued to speak so earnestly I began to think, "What is this? He seems to be very concerned about something, what does he want? He is so upset—there are tears in his eyes." In this agitated spill of French words, I began to catch the words 'mort' and 'Kennedy' and 'assassin'.

With his eyes boring seriously into mine, he is pumping my hand in a heartfelt handshake and repeating, "Le president, assassin, mort!" He must think I'm a simpleton as it begins to dawn on me

247

what he's saying. I realize I have been smiling and I think to myself, "Stop grinning this is BAD!" I can feel my face falling slowly into a serious, confused expression as I hear myself numbly saying, "Merci, merci, merci".

I turn the pram around and go straight back to the apartment. It's only midafternoon but I hear the elevator and my husband's footsteps in the outer hall. He's home early. Those are not his usual jaunty footsteps, they sound different—heavy and slow. His knock on our door is a thud. I open it. My young husband looks like a haggard old man. He says, "Kennedy's been shot in Dallas. He's dead."

We were in shock. We felt as if a lifeline to our country had been severed.

My husband went out to find an English newspaper and found a London Times and a Christian Science Monitor. The embassy flags were already at half-mast.

The next day we went out and saw all the flags were at half-mast. 'The Memorial to the Unknown American Soldiers' was engulfed in flowers. Strangers came up to us and shook our hands. Everyone had tears in their eyes. We did too. They were so 'moved,' so kind. I thought we had been invisible, but the neighborhood had known all along that we were the 'Americans.'

From that day on, neighborhood people greeted me with, "Bonjour Madame!" and a big, hearty Belgian handshake. They even leaned over and shook the baby's little hand, and soon she was saying "jouri" in return. "Jouri" was the third word she'd learned after "mama and dada".

Jing-Shio Su

I came to the United States from Taiwan in 1977 to pursue my American dream—earning a degree in Mathematics. I spent six years in the graduate school at the University of New Mexico in Albuquerque working on two Masters Degrees. My first degree was in Early Childhood Education, which was an extension of my college major, Home Economics. The second one was in Applied Mathematics. This degree gave me the opportunity to enter the software industry and explore the western culture.

After graduate school, I came to the Bay Area and started my career as a software engineer in 1983. For twenty-four years while developing my career, I was also busy raising a family. While my kids were in primary school, in 1995 I started a home-based math tutoring business as my weekend hobby.

In 2007, my high-tech career got to a point that made me re-think what I really wanted for myself. The decision was to leave the industry to fulfill my interest in teaching and to find something different that I might enjoy.

I slowly opened my weekday schedule for tutoring and filled my morning and early afternoon hours by line dancing, Ikebana and other activities. It took me five years to establish my semi-retired life style. As the daily routines became steady, I realized there was one thing missing – to polish my writing skill. Writing was always my least favorite subject in school, but I was doing well writing emails for work. The idea of looking for an opportunity to practice writing came to my mind, and that was the beginning of my memoir journey.

In the middle of one night in 2011, I was so bored that watching TV was one way to kill time. After the program I was watching ended, I saw a very dull TV advertisement about our memoir class. The screen was kind of grey (not colorful at all) with a simple box containing the key words "Saratoga Senior Center" and "Memoir/Writing".

Saratoga Senior Center, how convenient! Writing, wasn't that exactly what I had been thinking? Guess what! That simple boring TV advertisement brought me to our memoir group, and the family atmosphere of our memoir class has kept me going and encouraged me to "write" in "English". I realized that a story of my life can be small, but it can be very meaningful to people around me, even to those around the world.

Teacher Wu
My Fifth and Sixth Grade Teacher

by Jing-Shio Su

I grew up in Nantou, a very small town in the middle of Taiwan. For my generation and most of the families in my home town, academic performance was the number one task for all students. Studying hard, passing extremely difficult entrance exams to go to good schools, and obtaining a college degree with popular majors was a straight-forward way to be able to earn a living better than our parents.

I am the second child and second daughter of my parents. Having an older sister (two years older) made me less desirable to my grandparents. Having a very smart sister, I had been an ugly duckling since early childhood. Before fifth grade, I was an unimpressive student. In kindergarten, I could count only up to 29. In third grade, I could not memorize times tables. Very often, I felt I was a mediocre student and could never stand out no matter how hard I tried.

Teacher Wu was my teacher for two years, fifth and sixth grades. Unlike teachers of other fifth/sixth grade classes, he looked very kind and friendly. I felt very comfortable going to school since day one of fifth grade. Even though I continued to be an average student, I never felt I was much worse than other smart classmates on academic performance. While lots of

Teacher Wu

classmates were working hard and doing well, I barely managed to keep up with the curriculum. Even so, I still enjoyed going to school every day. Very often, Teacher Wu would ask me to go to school offices or other classes to deliver or pick up something for our class. I was a little helper/messenger and felt it was a great honor. I started to feel I was not who I had been before. Instead, I was capable and useful.

Entering sixth grade, I continued to be a helper, but in a different aspect. For some reason, I impressed Teacher Wu so much that he believed I could explain the processes of solving math problems in front of the class. I became a "little substitute teacher" even though he was not absent. He would sit at his desk in the corner of the classroom and watch me taking his place as a teacher. I was shy, but I was not afraid of standing in front of the class because I knew I understood the materials well enough to "teach" my classmates. Gradually I became more comfortable in that role, and

Nantou Elementary School, in my home town, Nantou, in the middle of Taiwan. This picture is of all the teachers taken in front of the office building 51 years ago for our year book when we graduated. In front of the tree is the open field where we had our daily assembly. The tree is a symbol of the school. Mr. Wu is in the back row far right with striped tie.

soon I found the experience enjoyable. I could tell that Teacher Wu was very happy with my performance. One day after I finished explaining a math solution, he told me: "You will be a great teacher when you grow up." As a result of the unique experiences, my math grade started to shine and solving tough math problems became a very exciting activity to me. That was the time when I started to develop my interest in mathematics.

During those two years, I gradually built my confidence and enjoyed the school curriculum so much that I passed the very tough entrance exam to an excellent girls' school (the Taichung Girls' School) where I spent six years, grade seven to grade twelve, before going to college. I had great math teachers every year and continued to shine in math curriculum in the girls' school. With the experiences of being a little substitute for Teacher Wu, I started to realize that I wanted to be a teacher when I grew up. After high school, I passed another major entrance exam to a special four-year college from which I graduated with a teaching credential for grades seven to twelve.

After college, I had options of either returning to my home town or staying in Taipei to pursue my dream job as a teacher. I visited Teacher Wu and asked him for advice. He recommended that I stay in Taipei, capital of Taiwan, for better career opportunities. I spent two years as a full-time teacher, and figured out that I wanted something more than just being a teacher. Being a teacher only fulfilled part of my interests; teaching math was what I really wanted for my life. In order to be able to achieve that goal, I needed an advanced degree in math, and that was the trigger that brought me to the United States.

I am extremely thankful that I met Teacher Wu before it was too late for me to learn to excel. He has been my mentor and my hero in several aspects. On several occasions, I went back to him seeking advice about some critical decisions in my life. I have been trying to carry out his legacy as a teacher in my math tutoring program by identifying the potential in each of my students and

253

using individualized approaches in teaching in order to maximize the potential of every one of them.

Teacher Wu had a profound influence on my life. I am very grateful for all that he did for me, and I miss him.

Note: Teacher Wu has passed away. I have translated this write-up into Chinese and given a copy to Mrs. Wu.

My Dream Watch

by Jing-Shio Su

For my generation and where I come from, a small town (Nantou) in the middle of Taiwan, having a watch was a luxury for school children. At the same time, life style was nothing like it is now. People got up, went to work or school, mothers went to the market daily for groceries. At the end of the day when everyone returned home, a hearty warm dinner was on the table for a family gathering. The routine was very simple; not having a watch was not an issue.

Going to middle school was a significant milestone for everyone in my families. To get into a good middle school was something the teacher, the school, the family and even the entire town would be very proud of. There was a tradition on my mother's side of the family. Uncles and Aunts would buy a watch for every sixth grade niece or nephew who was to enter middle school.

Knowing the family tradition, I could not help dreaming about what kind of watch I would like to have. My preference was a small, slim and feminine looking watch. Practicality had never been part of the considerations. Maybe I should say a watch was a piece of jewelry, not something to help me keep track of time. It was impolite to ask my aunts and uncles for a particular style of watch. All I could do was to wait and find out when I got it.

During my sixth grade year, I was having fun studying for the entrance exam to the best girls' school in Taichung, a town about a one hour bus ride away. Going to school and attending extra curriculum after school, I enjoyed the routine and was looking forward to receiving my first watch.

The two-day entrance exam took place in early July. While waiting for the result anxiously, I was also imaging what kind of watch I might get. The result of the exam came out in August. I was admitted to the girls' school. The excitement of the good news was soon replaced by the anxiety of getting my first watch. I knew the waiting for my first watch was about to end.

One afternoon, uncles and aunts came to my house. I knew I was getting the watch. Aunts, uncles and every one of my family sat down in our living room. The oldest brother of my mother handed me a beautiful box. Inside the box was the watch I had been waiting for. I opened the box and saw a classic, medium size watch, very suitable for a middle school girl. It was not as small as I wished. I was not sure if my facial expression was proper or not. But I do remember how disappointed I was at that moment. Knowing exchanging the watch was impossible, I politely thanked them for the gift.

During the six years at the girls' school, three years for middle school and three years for high school, the watch moved around with me every day. I relied on it heavily so I would not miss the 6:45 bus to school in the morning, the 4:45 bus to come home in the afternoon. The discounted student monthly pass only allowed me to take buses on those fixed schedules. The consequence of missing any of those two, I would have to pay for the regular ticket which was very costly for my parents. Every evening, I checked the time often to make sure I completed the homework, studied for the exams, going to bed on time. Especially my last year of high school, it helped me to manage my time effectively. The watch had made it possible for me to stay on track preparing for the entrance exam to a four-year college. That was when I realized I could not live without a watch. After high school, I got admitted to my dream college that offered free tuition, free room and board, degree with teaching credential (seven to twelve grades) and a teaching job.

During college, I shared my feeling and disappointment about my first watch with my mother. Several years later when I achieved my American dream of getting a graduate degree in math, my mother bought me a very nice gold tone Seiko watch as a graduation gift. It was smaller than my first one, but still not as feminine as I would like. I believe it must have cost her good part of her savings. So I do appreciate her thoughtfulness.

Finding my dream watch remained in my mind for a good 30 years. About ten years ago, I finally found one. When I first spotted it, I was afraid it was too small as I had started to experience the need for reading glasses. I took a quick look to make sure I was able to tell the time without reading glasses. After checking the return policy, I paid and took it home happily. At the age of early fifty, I finally got my dream watch. Since then I have developed other preferences and have other watches, but it is still my favorite one.

Can I Speak English?

by Jing-Shio Su

Can I speak English? Yes and no. Most of time, I think I know English well enough to be able to move around comfortably. But to some people, I may not be able to speak English just because my name is very Chinese.

I am from Taiwan and came to the States in the summer of 1977 to pursue graduate studies. I have to admit I was not able to speak English then, even though I had studied it in school for seven years, earned my Bachelor degree, and passed the TOEFL (Test of English as a Foreign Language) exam.

My journey with learning English started at the age of twelve. It was a daily class, six times a week, for six years from grade seven to grade twelve. (We had school for five and half days every week). Starting with writing alphabets including print, cursive, lower case, and upper case, the curriculum quickly moved to spelling, phonics and vocabulary followed by short, then long sentences and reading articles. Rules in grammar and phonics, together with tons of exceptions, were overwhelming for me. Subjects, verbs, nouns, especially prepositions made me wonder why I could read/write Chinese without learning Chinese grammar. Since it was new and an extremely important subject, I studied very hard and aced it all the time.

Because my Bachelor degree was in Home Economics, I chose to major in Early Childhood Education, a field in Home Economics, hoping that staying with the similar major would make my learning easier. It did not take me long to realize that I was in an English only environment at school. Can you imagine my first meeting with the foreign student advisor? I was able to understand some greeting words and managed to introduce myself. I felt comfortable because the advisor was helpful and made me feel I was welcome as one of the very few foreign students.

The real challenge came when school started in August. English text books, English lectures, English homework and reports, plus English quizzes and exams were daunting. But I was *brave* enough to stay calm and accept the challenges because that was something I had to overcome in order to fulfill my dream of earning an advanced degree. I worked as hard as I could and completed the degree in two years. I did not think I had done well in terms of academic performance, but I had endured the language challenges. I believed I came out much stronger and more comfortable exploring the culture and opportunities. The experiences of those two years have had significant impact on me and made it possible for me to be who I am today.

Actually part of the difficulty I encountered was due to my weakness in reading comprehension in general, not just in English. I could work with lots of numbers and make sense out of them, but I was not even able to write a good book report in Chinese after reading a Chinese book. Language has always been my most difficult subject. Writing has been something I would avoid as much as possible.

During my first two years in the states, I have to admit I was *not* able to speak English. A better way to say the same thing is 'I was able to speak broken English.' Luckily, the situation started to improve when I began to be surrounded by numbers in my daily routine at work. After earning the first degree, I got a job in the Waste Water Department of the City of Albuquerque as a chemistry analyst. On the job, we did lots of chemical experiments to test samples of the waste water collected from various spots in the city. Measuring cups, test tubes, and the results of chemical reactions all involved numbers which I could understand easily. With the security of being surrounded by numbers, I slowly felt more comfortable speaking English.

Starting the third year, I even explored real estate investment. From having zero knowledge about mortgage to become a proud property owner, I had lots of fun working with the numbers involved in the process. Listing price, purchase price, down payment, mortgage, principal, interest rate, APR, monthly payment and due day are nothing but numbers. Comparing to the fun of working with numbers, the legal aspect of the process was nowhere near scary.

While working full time, I continued going to school pursuing my American dream, getting a degree in mathematics. From Calculus up to all courses to fulfill the requirements for a Master's degree in math, "English" never got in the way. I realized my English was not too "broken" at all. As a student in the math department, my learning experiences were completely different. What a relief! Math statements, equations, and formulas say a lot without English. Surrounded increasingly by numbers, I gradually built my confidence to continue my journey in the states. I even earned a scholarship that required teaching one to two courses each semester. I was extremely comfortable lecturing math in 'English' in front of twenty-five to forty students. I believe I was able to speak English for the entire duration while studying math.

After completing the degree in math at the end of 1982, I moved to the Bay Area starting my career as a software engineer. Other than the expected adjustments to the work force of industry, I merged into the high-tech environment smoothly and developed my interests in the telecommunication industry. By that time, there was no doubt that I was able to speak English.

The daily routines as a working mother continued, and I thought English was almost a part of me until a call from an inexperienced insurance agent arrived. The agent tried to get my attention regarding my policy and sell me other products. As usual, I entertained the call by listening and responding kindly. While I had to pause to think about how to continue the conversation, instead of waiting patiently for my reply, he said, "You cannot speak English. I will ask my manager to give you a call. She is also a Chinese," and hung up.

He claimed I was not able to speak English, mainly because my name is very Chinese and I was not responding fast enough. Guess what! His manager was someone I had known for several years before the incident.

"Can I speak English?" I asked myself. "Of course," I answered. Not only that, I believe I can speak English very fluently when the subject matter is something I am most interested or familiar. A good example would be, "teaching math".

Phone Book

by Jing-Shio Su

We may be the last generation who uses the paper Phone Book. Remember the heavy, thick, yellow/black phone book delivered to your front door every year. The book was so heavy that I used it for weight while I prepared some pickled Chinese vegetables.

My husband and I came to the states in 1977 for advanced degrees with very little money. We needed to save money whenever possible. Since having a phone is absolutely necessary, getting a phone with no additional options and features has been our choice. This means my husband's name has been listed in the white page (residential section of the phone book) because removing it would cost additional money.

After spending six years in Albuquerque, New Mexico where we met most of our new friends in the states, we moved to San Jose to start our careers as engineers. For the five years when we lived in San Jose, a few friends from Albuquerque found us through the Phone Book. Therefore, having our name listed was a great advantage on top of saving money.

In 1987, we moved to Saratoga and continued to subscribe to AT&T land line with basic service, name listed, no caller ID, no call interrupt, and no call forwarding. Although the service was similar, living in Saratoga gave us a totally different experience.

Not too long after we settled in this small town, I got a call about my overdue balance on my credit card. It was the beginning of countless calls spread over several years.

One of my disciplines is paying off my credit card balances monthly all the time (assuming I did not forget about it). There were a few times I missed the deadline and was charged interest and late fee, but I always managed to get them removed by claiming I had been a loyal customer who paid off monthly balances. Therefore, I was certain I had no overdue balance.

The calls arrived from a so called 'collection agent'. He was looking for someone with the same last name as ours and lived in Saratoga. He must be very sure we were the people he was looking for. At first I was a little bit worried that I might have missed something. Being a working mother with two little kids, I simply did not have time to pay much attention to this issue other than answering the calls and carrying on the conversations. I refused to pay the amount due and was entertaining the collection agent enough number of times, my case was then given to a lawyer who called and threatened to take me to court. He must have been extremely frustrated that I would not admit I owed the money.

During those calls, the collection agent was trying to get my address, but I was alert enough to reply politely that he should have my address if I were the individual he was looking for. On the final call, I was informed I would receive a package from court. I wondered how the court would send me papers without my address. As expected, the court papers never arrived.

On one of the calls, I managed to get the bank name and a portion of the account number. I called the bank and found that we have never had any account with that bank.

I believe this issue started because my husband's name is listed in the Phone Book and we were the only Su listed at that time. Even though I endured this experience, I still did not regret it. Instead, I learned how a collection agency collects overdue balances. It is something I could never experience unless it is a mistake. It was a very unusual experience. I was proud of myself for handling this calmly and getting something positive out of it.

Stop Sign

by Jing-Shio Su

A stop sign is white on red and in the shape of an octagon. It requires a person to stop completely before proceeding. This is Driving Rule number one for people like me who came to the states after growing up without any driving experience. Where I come from, Taiwan, owning a car was a privilege for the extremely wealthy. Most people moved around by walking or bicycling in town, bus or train for going out of town.

Not too long after arriving in Albuquerque, New Mexico in 1977, I realized that I would not be able to do some essential daily routines, like grocery shopping, without a car. Taking public transportation is not very practical in the states. Owning a car and being able to drive was an exciting adventure while learning to drive was an arduous task.

Getting a ticket for not stopping 'completely' – does this sound familiar?

I got a traffic ticket on my birthday while I was pregnant with my first child. Like other working women in the Bay Area, I was running around trying to get to some place in a rush on a Sunday afternoon. It was at an intersection in North San Jose. I stopped and checked if it was safe to turn right. Being able to see the street clearly – no car in the distance, I made a right turn. Not too long after turning, I noticed a policeman behind me with his lights flashing. I knew I needed to stop. The policeman issued me a traffic

264

citation for not stopping completely. Being confused, scared and inexperienced in handling such a situation, I did not know what to do other than accept the ticket. Based on that instance, I stopping and then proceeding safely were not sufficient. The stop has to be a *complete* stop. I still do not know what a complete stop means, but my interpretation is the speedometer should say 'zero' as a numerical reference. Since then, I always stop and wait for the speedometer to be at zero and then take off slowly to ensure the stop is 'complete.' But the way I 'stop' gets somewhat annoying to people driving behind me.

Stop sings can be missed easily due to mature trees or bushes at the corner of an intersection. So, watching for these unnoticeable stop signs has become another one of my routines so I will be able to avoid a 'stop sign' related driving citation. Driving in a neighborhood I would make sure there is no hidden stop sign. I also learned that stop signs are usually placed on minor streets.

One summer, my friend, who lived nearby, needed a ride home. I thought I knew her neighborhood well enough that getting to her place should not be an issue. Even though it is near where I live, it is in an area I have never been. On the way home while I was driving on a street off of Prospect Road, I considered it as a major street compared to others branching off from it. Therefore, watching for a stop sign did not enter into my mind. All of a sudden, I realized that I was in the middle of an intersection where a big SUV was arriving from the right and was not stopping. I promptly stopped and turned back to see if I should have stopped. Yes, I did miss a stop sign.

The SUV stopped and a 'gentleman' got out. I rolled down my window and prepared to apologize. Before I even had a chance to say something, he asked, "Do you know the stop sign has been in place for forty some years? Do you live here?" My honest answer was no for not knowing the stop sign was there and yes for I do live nearby. After I sincerely apologized, he got back into his SUV and wanted me to drive ahead. I insisted to let him go first. Then we were on the same road until Prospect. I purposely turned right knowing it will not take me home just to avoid driving right behind him.

Stop signs can be anywhere. To be safe, one should always watch for one and stop 'completely' all the time before proceeding.

Every Other Day

by Jing-Shio Su

We all know there are seven days in a week. What is special about seven? It is an odd number. What is special about seven being an odd number? Since seven is an odd number, 'every other day' in a week can be four days: 'Monday, Wednesday, Friday, and Sunday' or three days: 'Tuesday, Thursday, and Saturday'.

To remember to do something 'every other day', one would have to ask: "Did I do it yesterday?" If the answer is 'yes', you would not need to do it today. It sounds very simple, but it is no longer a simple question as I am getting older. The deficiency in my memory has made it more and more difficult to remember what I did or did not do yesterday. Therefore to do things every other day has not been easier over the last several years. While we are so used to the fact that there are seven days in a week, I had a horrible experience with the odd seven.

The experience started with having a pair of parakeets, one green and the other blue. They are my husband's pets. Chien feeds them, cleans the cage, and buys their food. I would become the default caretaker when he is out of town. Most of the time, I have been the beneficiary of having them. Since they make noise when the house is quiet, they are good

267

company when I am home alone. They also make noise wanting to join the conversation when I talk on the phone using speaker or have friends over. Their noise can be so loud that I have to leave the room or move their cage to the other room and shut the doors behind to be able to continue the conversations.

For the first several years, I had no trouble taking care of (feeding) them while my husband was out of town. When I got home after work, they would try to get my attention by making loud noises. My routine was to make sure they had enough food and feed them when needed. It worked well and had never caused any issue. In 2007, I left my last industry job and became a stay home mom. Being at home most of the time every day, their noise slowly became unnoticeable.

Chien traveled for business as usual. For some reason, he reminded me to feed the birds 'every other day' before he took off for one of his business trips in 2009. That was the first time I realized the birds had been fed every other day by their primary caretaker, my husband. The instruction was very clear and sounded very simple. For the first couple days, I was on track and the birds were happy. My daily routines continued – teaching, line dancing, gardening, etc. But I started to realize I had trouble following the routine of feeding the birds 'every other day.' I thought I was doing okay until one afternoon, several days after Chien left, I noticed the birds were very quiet. "Did I feed the birds? When was the last time I fed them?" I asked myself. I did not have a definite answer. I ran to the cage and what I was afraid of had happened. One of the birds was lying on the bottom of the cage. It had died! I felt guilty as I thought that I was entirely at fault because I had not figured out how to feed them 'every other day.' I promptly drove to Petco and bought another bird of the same color. The cashier not only collected the money for the new bird, but also asked me to sign a contract promising to take good care of the new bird. I looked at the cashier and asked, "Is this something I need to sign every time I buy a pet?" "Yes", the cashier answered authoritatively. While I was suffering the guilt that my bird might have died of hunger, I felt uneasy signing.

Over the last 13 plus years, we have been having two parakeets. About six months ago, one of them died while Chien was in town. Since he has been the primary caretaker, he thought the bird died because it was very old. This instance made me think the bird under my care in 2009 potentially died of aging also. Even though I do not remember how long we had that bird, I knew we had had it for a very long time.

Chien still travels very often. I learned to ignore his instruction of feeding the birds every other day. Instead, I would try to feed them every day. By doing so, I have a sustainable routine that I do not need to ask myself, "Did I feed the birds yesterday?" Over the last several years, our two parakeets get fed 'every other day' when their primary caretaker is around. Otherwise, the feeding schedule is 'every day.'

Pink Lady Mabel

by Jing-Shio Su

I first met Mabel at our memoir class in 2011. From the story she shared in my first memoir class, I wrote down "BE YOURSELF" and "GO AHEAD." Even though I do not remember her story, I am sure I caught those two phrases for a reason.

Both, "BE YOURSELF" and "GO AHEAD" take confidence and courage. Back then, I was not sure how I would stay in the class due to lack of confidence in my writing. Inspired by Mabel's story, I told myself, "Be Me" and "Try It Out." One thing I was very sure of was, if I did not give it a try, I would regret it. To chicken out was for sure not an option.

My first story, Teacher Wu, was completed and shared in November 2011. Even with only one story, I knew I could and was comfortable to stay. Every story shared by others in the class inspired me and gave me ideas about what I could write. I learned the stories do not have to be "big." I gradually completed several more stories including "My Father," "Every Other Day," "Phone Book" and several others.

My close friendship with Mabel started with her sharing a book of Chinese Jade with me. The book was from her Chinese neighbor who lived by Mabel for many years before she moved back to Taiwan. I got chances to stop by Mabel's apartment a few times. She liked pink and called herself, "Pink Lady." I brought her a simple flower bouquet of carnations on every visit. Pink carnations were the top choice in general, but orange or peach for Halloween, red for Christmas, and yellow for some Easters were also great choices. No matter which color I chose, Mabel loved all of them.

In her living room, there was a chair next to the patio door. Sitting on the chair, she could watch TV, look at the wall units with her collections of pottery and china, and enjoy the sun coming in from the patio door. Next to the chair, there was an end table where she put books, magazines and pictures. The carnations would be placed on the end table so she could enjoy the fresh flowers all the time. There were times we chatted a little bit before I left.

The other place to meet Mabel was the Saratoga Safeway. I was used to looking for her car every time I shopped there. I spotted her car a couple times. I always made an effort to find her in the store and check if she needed any help. Her reply was always, "I got to be able to do this by myself." That was our Mabel, very independent.

When I offered to bring her another arrangement of fresh carnations toward the end of last year, she told me that she was having a hard time adding water to the glass to keep the flowers fresh. From the last visit prior to that conversation, I noticed she had trouble getting up from the chair and then walking to the kitchen. I continued to call her every once in a while. The last two times were to get her stories for our book and to wish her well prior to her major dentist appointment to have her tooth removed.

Busy spending time with my 88-year-old father, I did not get a chance to talk to her during this summer. I missed the opportunity to visit her while she was in the hospital. Deb's sad e-mail arrived when I was in Taiwan. I came home and realized that I can no longer visit her. So I wrote to capture some of my memories of Mabel. In memory of Mabel, I made a bouquet of pink carnations in her favorite green glass.

271

Dick Walthart

I started writing my memoirs after beginning Louise Webb's class about a year ago, after I first learned about it in the Saratoga Senior Center's newsletter. I first met Louise at an art class she helped put on at the activity center. The memoirs class is similar to a poetry writing workshop I was in many years ago.

The memoirs group is comprised of older people with a common interest in writing and I appreciate the group dynamics. Some of the more interesting members are Chuck, who has a whimsical style; Anne, who writes lyrical nature pieces about her native Sweden; and Luanna, who apparently gets ideas for her mystery-tinged stories while working a window cleaning day job.

I was born in Hollywood, California and have been married for 58 years to the same woman. We have two adult sons. Our family moved to the San Jose area after I got a job transfer to a technical writer position, but my main career was as a social worker professional with the Santa Clara County Department of Social Services (Family and children's division). I am currently retired.

I find that the discipline of expressing myself in writing helps me better understand myself and my situation by putting them in perspective. I also have an interest in politics as a hobby.

Out of the Woods

by Dick Walthart

In the early 80s we first met in a late afternoon therapy group. She, depressed by her estranged husband's infidelity while she was pregnant, and me still running from the major depression I had suffered after my mother's death many years previously-which had tapped the negative side of my ambivalence towards her. Depression can be thought of as anger turned inwards, having a numbing effect which deadens the senses and reduces ones inner life to a bleak world devoid of softer emotions.

I had shown up for some of the therapy sessions in construction work clothes, since I had taken a three month leave of absence from my county social worker job in order to do some physical work to relieve stress.

After therapy, the group would gather at a hippy girl's place where we socialized, including some pot smoking. I remember our first slow dance, where it felt like her body was actually melting into mine.

She was Irish-Catholic, with the same first name as my mother; and I recall her saying in my parked car as I was caressing her breasts, that her mother had told her as a teenager, "No petting below the waist."

Things didn't go any further until one day she asked if I would like to go for an outing over to the coast with her.

I took that day off from work, and in the morning we met in a Los Gatos parking lot and left in my car.

273

It was a sunny day, and we took a side trip to a Santa Cruz grocery store where she bought some sandwich makings and soda pop; then we continued up the coast past the "Red, White, and Blue" nude beach towards Half Moon Bay.

After passing some salt marshes with herons and other scenic spots, we stopped at a turn-out overlooking the ocean and had our lunch.

Afterwards, heading back down the coast, we stopped at a restaurant I knew of with an ocean view and had some wine and cheese and a long conversation.

Leaving there in the late afternoon, we were on the road again with her sitting close beside me on the front seat.

Feeling drawn to her, I rested my hand on her thigh and she breathlessly whispered, "Pull over."

I took the next exit inland, finally finding an isolated area where we parked off the road among some trees, and commenced some unhurried and purposeful petting below the waist which felt at once magical and a little like playing doctor.

She was unusually quiet and when I asked about this she admitted to feeling some guilt. I put my arm around her shoulders and she noticeable relaxed. We then shared a mellow time for the rest of the way back.

Upon parting in the parking lot she kissed me fully on the mouth.

In the subsequent months, whenever I could manage it from my in-the-field-job, I would stop by her place of work (she supervised a small chain bookstore) and we would go out for coffee.

Things eventually wound down and the last thing I remember about her was that she had remarried.

I've always been a sucker for a "damsel in distress" but, in retrospect, that day stands out for me as the turning point in a journey towards reclaiming my feelings.

An Old Man Learns a New Trick

by Dick Walthart

My preemptive grieving after my wife's fall
which punctuated her gradual decline
and left her semi-conscious in the hospital for three days
brought back my childhood tears
at a grade school performance of *Dying Swan*.
The spunky, upfront girl who wasn't my mother
(whose sudden death had led me to a major depression)
wasn't all there anymore
and my tough love approach to caretaking had overtones of
anger
heightened by our realigned roles and more contentious
communication.
After a while, my untethered affections transferred to another
woman,
soft-spoken, matter-of-fact and seemingly receptive
to my poetic advances, which she nicely side-stepped by
reframing them
as pretty words more suitably submitted elsewhere,
and so turned out to be a muse, lessening the spell while
inspiring in me a positive glow,
which I passed back to my wife, and began applying what I had
learned
about a lighter touch being called for in matters of the heart
and seeing her idiosyncrasies apart from her frailties
and appreciating them both
and breathing a sigh of relief, I smiled.

Poetry

by Dick Walthart

Summer Colors

Mellow yellow melts into me
-the warming sun-
Moving in waves, subsiding
While I tan slowly on the beach
Under a clear blue sky.

Truth in Presidential Campaigning

Which is worse, schoolyard bully b.s.
Or grudging semi-transparency?
This no-win choice suggests
Looking beyond character-driven politics
-guilty pleasure that this may be-
To focus on how and where the candidates would lead us.
One, crawling through a tunnel of self-interest and divisiveness
towards "greatness"?
Or, the other, walking a road of informed hope towards unity.

Bern Baby

Ode to Bernie Sanders, Democratic Presidential Candidate
(With apologies to Wm. Blake)

Pied piper, Bernie bright
will you lead us to the light?
Oh, what hand and what eye
formed thy fearful "pie in the sky"?

Poetry

by Dick Walthart

T Rump

Ode to Donald Trump, Republican Presidential Candidate

The Great White
is a barking fright
an ominous clown
with squinty eyes and frown
a snorting lout
with perpetual pout
a big baby
whose mama maybe
didn't look his way – be
enough (It's all about him/winning at any cost).

Clock Running

Ode to Hillary Clinton, Democratic Presidential Candidate

Hillary, Billary, Bern,
peoples' trust you must earn
transparency showing
to get our hearts glowing,
Hillary, Billary, Bern.

Topical Suggestions

If you get stuck and don't know what to write, here are some suggestions that may just trigger a thought or a memory.

Stories told to you about the day you were born.

Camping adventures.

Describe your parents, grandparents. What did they look like? Color of eyes, hair, complexion. How tall?

Any special memories with grandparent/s.

Where were your parents born? How old were they when they got married?

How many siblings do you have?

Where did you grow up?

Were you in the military? Where did you serve? What was your rank?

What is your occupation?

Special romances you will never forget.

Athletic abilities.

Favorite foods.

Travels in the United States or in other countries.

Did you have close cousins growing up?

Do you have a nickname and how did you get it?

What are your hobbies?

Any stories about riding a horse?

Did you live in the horse and buggy days?

Are you named after a relative?

Did you serve in a war while in the military?

What is your educational background?

What was the make and model of your first car? Was anything special about it?

Does your family have any "old sayings" they always repeat?

Does your family gather for holidays or game nights?

Were you bullied in school?

Were you a bully in school?

Did you have a favorite teacher?

Have you learned any important lessons in life? How did you learn them?

Do you like your first name and middle name? Were you named after someone?

Pets. How many pets have you had? Do you remember their names?

How many siblings do you have and where are you in order of birth.

How did you decide to name your children? What are their names and who are they named after?

Girlfriends, boyfriends?

How did you meet your spouse? Long or short engagement?

Do you enjoy yardwork? Why?

What is your favorite season and why?

What is your favorite holiday and why?

Did you have family vacations? What were they and which one was the best.

Did you or anyone in your family have a serious illness?

What do you do for relaxation?

What was your life like growing up?

Do you enjoy going to the movies? What is your favorite move of all time and why?

What was your first car? How old were you when you learned to drive?

Which do you like the best, the mountains or the ocean and why?

How far back do you know your family's genealogy?

Do you know your ethnicity on all sides of your family?

Have you ever written a book or want to?

How many homes have you lived in and do you remember the addresses?

Do you enjoy sports, bicycling, swimming, etc.?

What is your favorite garment you like to wear?

How many pairs of shoes do you have and why?

Are you technologically savvy?

Did you have a favorite toy while growing up?

Do you prefer to be inside or outside the house? Why?

Did you go to college and what did you study?

Favorite subject in high school.

Were you a joyful child or quiet and shy?

Is there a color that you absolutely hate and won't wear?

Would you rather read a book or go hiking?

Did you have a favorite pet? Why?

Have you taken a road trip? Where did you go?

Do you enjoy boating?

Did you have a lot of friends in school?

Did you have a best friend? Who was it and why?

Are you a religious person? Were you raised in church?

When did you start using a computer and a smart phone?

Do you drink coffee? How many times do you go to Starbucks in a week?

Did you ever attend summer camp? What was your experience?